D0106239

Meditation
in Motion

Books by the Author

THE EMERGENT SELF (coauthor)

THE PARTICIPANT SELF (coauthor)

APPROACHING THE SACRED: AN INTRODUCTION TO SPIRITUAL READING

STEPS ALONG THE WAY: THE PATH OF SPIRITUAL READING

A PRACTICAL GUIDE TO SPIRITUAL READING

THE JOURNEY HOMEWARD: ON THE ROAD OF SPIRITUAL READING

TELL ME WHO I AM (coauthor)

AM I LIVING A SPIRITUAL LIFE? (coauthor)

RENEWED AT EACH AWAKENING

PRACTICING THE PRAYER OF PRESENCE (coauthor)

CELEBRATING THE SINGLE LIFE: A SPIRITUALITY FOR SINGLE PERSONS IN
TODAY'S WORLD

CREATIVE FORMATION OF LIFE AND WORLD (coeditor)

BLESSINGS THAT MAKE US BE: A FORMATIVE APPROACH TO LIVING THE
BEATITUDES

PATHWAYS OF SPIRITUAL LIVING

Meditation
in Motion

SUSAN ANNETTE MUTO

IMAGE BOOKS
A Division of
Doubleday & Company, Inc.
Garden City, New York
1986

Excerpts from "Choruses from 'The Rock'" in *Collected Poems 1909–1962* by T. S. Eliot, copyright 1936 by Harcourt Brace Jovanovich, Inc.; copyright © 1963, 1964 by T. S. Eliot. Reprinted by permission of the publisher.

Library of Congress Cataloging-in-Publication Data

Muto, Susan Annette.
Meditation in motion.

I. Spiritual life—Catholic authors.   I. Title.
BX2350.2.M882   1986   248.3'4   86-4690
ISBN 0-385-23533-X (pbk.)

Contents

ACKNOWLEDGMENTS

With gratitude, I acknowledge the following persons without whose help I could not have completed the writing and publishing of this book: my colleagues, staff, and friends at the Institute of Formative Spirituality, most notably Father Adrian van Kaam, C.S.Sp., and Father Richard Byrne, O.C.S.O., along with our associate and adjunct professor, Father Jerome Vereb, C.P. Thanks are also due to my secretary, Carol Pritchard, and to my typist, Eve Bauer; to fellow members of the Epiphany Association; to Patricia Kossmann, senior editor at Doubleday; and, last but not least, to my family. It is to our mother, Mrs. Helen Muto, that I dedicate in a special way many of these words and the memories they evoke, which she alone can fully appreciate.

Duquesne University
January, 1986

To My Readers

Words rest inside a writer's mind waiting for the right moment to emerge. Those in this book have been germinating for a long time. The idea of writing about daily openings to meditation and prayer—whoever and wherever we may be—was born several years ago aboard a cruise ship from Miami to the Bahamas.

While on board I met a chaplain with whom I had a number of challenging conversations. He was Italian but traveled frequently to America. He loved this country and its people with their charming accents, their penchant for the biggest, the best, the tallest, their dynamism. But what fascinated him the most was the Americans' love for their cars: the time they spent cruising down the road; the thrill they felt in owning one or two shining vehicles; the money they squandered to repair them. American cars were luxurious by European standards. Generally, he observed, people drove them alone. Families rode together, of course; friends took a ride; couples enjoyed a rendezvous. But often he would notice one person sitting in a car, seemingly in meditation.

Conversations with the chaplain convinced me that there had to be a connection between our busy day and these still moments. I began to wonder if it was possible to meditate on any and all occasions, if one could live in an attitude of prayerful presence while being in one's car or on a plane, at home or in the office.

This experience led me to ask: Does meditation have to be squeezed in between the events of life, or can it be integrated into whatever we happen to be doing? Is it not true that presence to the divine mystery, amid the mundaneness of the everyday, is neither a burden nor an obligation but that which makes life meaningful? Clearly the idea of writing such a book stayed with me. What renewed my interest in it was a powerful memory of Frank Muto, my father.

For a number of years before his death, Dad drove a red station wagon, fondly tagged "Office on Wheels," "Old Trooper That Will Outlive Me," and other names only he knew. Behind the visor one might find his latest home-remodeling contract; invoices outstanding; gas-station receipts covering the past six months; one new and several used toothpicks; a black comb with three teeth missing but still able, as he said, to do the trick.

The visor on the passenger side seemed to be the best place to store maps and holy cards. It ceased to function as protection against the sun. Mother argued that maps belonged in the glove compartment, but Dad insisted that in the Wagon they belonged behind the visor—and that was that. The glove compartment did contain one pair of working gloves and everything else that did not fit behind the visor, important items like Polaroid sunglasses with one side clasp missing, but still wearable; several completed contracts; last year's gas receipts; a tube of lipstick in case Mom got desperate when she rode with him; a can opener; a straw; a penknife; an expired ticket for a free car wash for ladies on Tuesday afternoons; an address book; rosary beads; and several scraps of paper containing one-word messages like "Church," imperatives like "Call Joe today!", and various phone exchanges followed by cryptic initials like "M.O'P."

The passenger seat was clear except for a few not-to-be-discarded newspapers and magazines, which could, however, be rearranged as soon as one sat down. The backseat could be cleared too, provided that there was room left in the rear of the "Bomb," as my brother Victor christened it, to catch the overflow.

It was in the rear of the Wagon that Dad really got down to business, for it contained the serious tools of his trade: ladders; cans of paint; a bucket of brushes; the essential carpenter's kit; cleaning equipment; drop cloths; and, tucked behind the spare tire, a fishing rod and folding chair—Dad's way of ensuring that when work became too much he could take off and follow life's finer call to relax and meditate under the sun. There was still room for two blankets, an old hamper, night flares, and a water jug. In fact, as he himself said many times, the Wagon was his home away from home. It was work and life space rolled into one.

We lost count of the times the Bomb broke down, nearly ended up in the junkyard, and came back again to Candace Street repaired and ready to hit the road. Once when the Wagon fizzled out in the middle of a major highway and had to be towed home for the umpteenth time, Dad put his foot down and announced at dinner, "This is it. The Wagon has got to go!" Before the dawn of departure day, Mother caught him peeking out the front door, checking to see if the "Old Girl" was there, as if she had heard his threat and, like a lady offended, gone puffing down the street in a cloud of righteous anger.

That morning, as usual, Dad left the house, said a prayer, lifted the hood, tinkered with the motor, walked around the entire Wagon three times, and decided, to no one's surprise, "There's plenty of life in the Old Girl yet." Mother insisted that Dad spent at least as much money patching up the Old Girl as she spent on her

whole wardrobe. But then, she was sure, the Wagon was
her only competition for Dad's affection.

Periodically Dad's Office on Wheels got a new coat of
paint. The last color he chose was barn red, for the simple reason that he did not want to waste the paint left
over from a job he was doing for the owner of a race-
track. As he sprayed the paint on, it left a fine veneer
that covered most of the Wagon's cracks and dents. From
then on, it became a landmark on our street. I never gave
directions to the house without saying, "Look out for the
red wagon parked in front of it."

Only after Dad's death—and only because the insur-
ance payments were so high—did Mom call a garage to
haul the Wagon ever so gently away. The clearest proof
of Dad's departure from us remains to this day the
empty space in front of our house where the Old Girl
used to be.

The relationship between Dad and his Wagon was
more than physical (a transport vehicle); more than functional (an office on wheels). It was also spiritual (a faithful companion and friend). Some of Dad's best conversations took place between him and the Wagon and God.
He would analyze new customers on the way to meeting
them for the first time. He would work out his anger
when a tradesman tried to pull underhanded tricks, for
the one virtue he insisted on in business was honesty.

It was to the Wagon that he would confess his bouts of
bad temper; his worries about us children; his conviction
that he could never retire from the trade until God and
his body told him it was over. He prayed in the Wagon,
talked to himself, laid plans for the day, laughed at old
jokes, sang his favorite songs, cursed inefficient, careless
labor, ate lunch, protected himself from the rain, and
always came home in time for dinner. True, he had another, more comfortable car for long trips, but he never

bestowed upon it the affection reserved for the Wagon alone.

I do not think this experience of prayerful presence to one's occupation or situation belongs to Dad only. Many people, myself included, develop meditative relationships with their cars, their homes, their places of work. Prayer time becomes any time one is alone or with a friend, on a trip or in the garden, taking a walk or admiring a mountain. For example, people not only curse their cars when they break down or praise them for good performance; they also muse in them; remember good times and bad; drift through past, present, and future scenarios; meditate in the lost moments they spend at stop signs and traffic signals; relish their solitude; and pray.

During times of transport from here to there, a car can be like a little cave on wheels, not as stark as a desert hermitage but no less a place where one can be alone. Switching off radio or tape recorder, I find that my car provides a space in which I can listen to the silence, behold nature in seasonal splendor, worship my Maker, welcome the dawn, let daylight business drone softly into dark, quiet evening hours.

A lot of people have told me that they can think best in their cars. This is another instance of the way in which meditation can be integrated into whatever we happen to be doing. Drives to and from work offer us an opportunity to be alone or to plan our day, to stay silent or to talk to God. Because human beings are innately transcendent, it seems safe to say that whatever they do has a spiritual potential. What, therefore, helps or hinders our ability to pray always? Can we live in prayer without leaving the world?

While I'll be sharing many of my own experiences in response to these questions, I have found that what is unique for one of us contains universal truths for all. To be spiritual means to be open to reality in its deepest ground. Religion is our relationship to the sacred. Spiritual formation means being receptive to the "more than" in the midst of the mundane. Accepting and coping with reality, while being open to the mystery that gratuitously sustains and permeates our lives, enables us to meditate at every moment.

In the following chapters, I shall try to support this claim by responding further to such key questions as: How can one be more sensitive to the movements of the Spirit in the events that compose each day? What are the ways and means of integrating our inner life with our everyday commitments to family, community, and society at large? In a world where people complain increasingly of feeling fragmented, alienated, and isolated, where drug addiction and alcoholism are on the rise, can we allow spirituality to remain the luxury of a religious elite, or must it become a survival measure for all?

It is my contention that wholeness and holiness cannot remain the exclusive domain of monks and ministers, gurus and mystics. Harmonious living must be possible for the average person in the midst of the world. Rather than focusing on that which divides us from ourselves and one another, we have to bring to light that which unites. We have to draw spirituality down from the mountaintop of monastic concerns into the marketplace.

Amid the current information explosion, amid the rapid expansions of contemporary consciousness, we need to recover the vision of a balanced, wise, and wholesome spiritual life—a vision in which faith and formation, contemplation and action, solitude and service blend together for the betterment of humankind and the world.

Throughout this book, I will attempt to respond by way of counsel, story, and reflection to the real need of people to experience the transcendent in their here-and-now situation as well as in their response to the global needs of humanity. I hope this book will, in a modest way, contribute to the efforts of concerned men and women throughout the world to find a distinctively human spirituality, one that manifests respect and understanding for each member of every religion, culture, and tradition, however diverse. Such love, and the prayerful presence that arises from it, must prevail for the sake of establishing lasting justice, peace, and mercy on our planet.

1
Food for Thought

OPENING MEDITATION

Close your eyes for a moment. Think of one event that happened to you today, this week, or during the past month that really touched your heart. Call this event to mind as vividly as possible. It may be a sad or joyful encounter, a humorous exchange, a warm greeting on a cold day. Move back into this moment as fully as imagination will allow. Meditate on it. Let the event give rise to reflection. What is its meaning for you? Why did it touch your heart? Think about it for a while, thank God for it, and, if you wish, record the event and your responses to it in your journal. Then, let this personal experience remain with you as you read this chapter.

To be in touch with oneself, to be still, to listen attentively, to think—these common events evoke meditation. The spiritual life calls us from time to time to step off the speeding train of existence and assess our direction. We need to ask ourselves such questions as: Who am I most deeply? What has become of my youthful ideals? Am I in tune with my sacred origins? Is life slipping through my fingers day by day, or does it have some purpose? Am I using my gifts and talents to the fullest? I need to ponder these questions not once a year on retreat but as part of my daily routine.

I find myself drawn to this type of meditation when I am driving alone. In the car by myself, there is nothing to do but drive carefully. Provided that I resist the adolescent urge to turn transportation into a competition, a race to beat the next car to the corner, I can use this time as a chance to be more in touch with the overall direction of my life.

Human beings are mysterious creatures. We are born into a particular society, but we are not programmed instinctively, like ants or bees, to support its survival. Our behavior can be constructive or destructive. We rely on bodily senses to respond to certain stimuli, but through the powers of reason, mind, and will, we can go beyond sensate perception. We take pride in creative productivity. We lament the loss of natural and human resources. Our ultimate dignity rests not on the quantity of our achievements but on the quality of our lives. There is in us an insatiable quest for the "more than," a driving, transcendent energy that pushes us beyond earthbound limits to the exploration of new potential.

It is wonderful to spend what might otherwise be lost moments, as when we are alone in our car, on these and similar reflections. Rather than take for granted the major and minor events that happen on our journey through life, we allow them to provide us with food for thought. What happens can give way to new yet familiar insights or shock us out of complacency into unaccustomed spheres of self-awareness. Let me share one such experience with you.

I can recall using as an example in talks the case of a person who goes to the doctor for a routine checkup, only to be told that something is seriously the matter that may require exploratory surgery. This example is no longer theoretical. It is real, for it happened to me.

I had returned home from a long trip during which I had been too busy traveling and speaking to concentrate on the few health problems I was having, attributing them to the usual sicknesses a different pace and diet can cause. When I felt no better, I decided it was time to see a doctor. I had a vague feeling from the mumbled remarks he made to his nurse that I was in some kind of trouble, but I was unprepared for his diagnosis. The problem area he examined revealed suspicious-looking tissue that in his opinion required immediate surgery, followed by a detailed pathology report. My God! What did he mean by "suspicious"? There could be an indication of malignancy. We had to find out quickly.

The exam took place on a Monday morning, and for the next week my life seemed to turn upside down. The specter of malignancy colored every other reality. In the face of that pronouncement, I began to sink into a dark night of sense and spirit. Life lost its usual color and drifted into a gray cloud of uncertainty. I could find no reason for what was happening. I was sharply aware of the mystery of life and of myself in the middle of it. This event compelled me to confront my finitude. The first person I phoned was my mother, who could barely speak because she was so concerned. In the end it was her courage and support that most sustained me as I related what had occurred to the rest of my family. I called friends and asked them to pray, but I still felt terribly alone, conscious in a painful way of all that had been and of what might now never be.

I shall always remember what it was like to be alone in my car after leaving the doctor's office. Life seemed surreal. Daily routines, not worth worrying about, like eating certain foods and avoiding others, loomed up in immense importance. Real concerns, like catching up on neglected correspondence, became utterly unimportant. Body and spirit were momentarily flung apart: the body portending its inevitable collapse, the spirit fighting to find some deeper meaning.

Unbelievable as it might seem, the night of the day I received the news, I had to be on a plane bound for St. Louis, where I was to begin a one-day conference for school principals and religious educators the following morning. The isolation of that evening overwhelmed me. Kind as the sisters who hosted me were, I found it impossible to communicate how miserable I felt.

After phoning my mother to see how she was and to share with her my hopes and fears, I went back to the small convent room where I was staying and for many hours past midnight wrestled with God. Only when I ceased seeking answers and began gradually to commend my spirit into His hands did I feel enough peace to fall asleep. The conference proceeded well, despite the weakness I harbored within. Where would I find the courage to face the unknown? Amazingly, I continued to function as a teacher, though my heart was heavy with concern.

A few days before I entered the hospital I asked someone whom I knew would understand my predicament to go with me for a walk. The person I would normally have consulted under such circumstances, a dear and supportive spiritual guide and friend, was out of the country. His absence was another cause for the aloneness that engulfed me like the humid August air. The walk was a partial remedy for my pain, for in the course of our conversation I discovered that my companion had gone through a similar death-in-life experience. He encouraged me to carry on, not with pious theory but with actual facts from his own ordeal before, during, and after a heart attack. He assured me that I could go through the upcoming operation because of the inner resources he saw in me. I would discover, as he did, that anger and loneliness were not signs of a lack of faith. It was normal to feel this way. What mattered was not suppressing my emotions under a veneer of spiritual verbiage but honestly telling God what I was going through. Then the sense of surrender I had felt that first night in St. Louis would gradually increase, and I could face this trauma with some semblance of grace.

At one point in our walk, a wounded baby robin hopped across the park path, its left wing weakened perhaps by a too-early push from the nest. My friend observed, "You feel like this little bird—so vulnerable, so fragile. But don't give way to the doubt that God doesn't hear your prayers and the prayers of everyone who is beseeching Him for you. He cares as much for you as for this tiny creature." It was as if God wanted to give me a symbol of hope, for no sooner had my friend spoken these words than the robin flapped its wings and flew, albeit with a wobble, to the lowest branch of a nearby tree. A small victory, to be sure, but it was enough to make me breathe a sigh of relief.

The day before I entered the hospital, while putting my office and apartment in some kind of order, I prayed over and over again, "O Lord, come to my assistance, O God, make haste to help me." In the passage of time from admission to the operation, I asked the Lord to calm my fears and to grant me the grace of which the poet George Herbert sings when he writes, "Affliction shall advance the flight in me." Finally, as I sank into the sleep of surgery, I found myself uttering in surrender the words of Sir Thomas Browne, "Thy will be done, though in my own undoing."

It is impossible to attain the heights of such self-understanding if one is not willing to plumb the depths of suffering. In ways I could neither have predicted nor willed, Holy Providence had led me to this point. I could do nothing but be present to the trauma of the event as it unfolded, trusting that the Lord would not try me beyond my strength to endure, that He would answer my voiced and voiceless prayers.

The surgery was on Friday and by the following Monday the report was back from the pathology division. The tissue removed was acutely enflamed, but there was no sign of malignancy. When I heard these words, it was as if a cool wave temporarily washed away the pain I was feeling. My prayers, and those offered by friends and family, were answered, but the questions I had asked throughout this week were so powerful that they left me a changed person. I had stood on the cutting edge between life and death, and, whatever the outcome, I could not forget that the finger of God had touched me.

The day I left the hospital my brother Victor, who himself had been worried sick, drove me home. We were both so grateful for the positive outcome of the operation that we could hardly speak. We could enjoy the ride in relative silence, content to be together in quiet thanksgiving. Everything was the same: the old and new parts of the city, the late August sky, the lovely green hills, the heavy, honeysuckle air; but everything was different, etched in finer detail, appreciated in its life-giving beauty, as if we were beholding it for the first time.

I loved that ride home from the hospital, prone on the backseat of the car, more than any I can remember. I knew a little more about who I was because I almost, in a manner of speaking, was not. I recall how much I enjoyed climbing out of the car, going into the apartment, talking to my mother and best friends, while remaining internally calm, not even trying to put into words what I was feeling. After everyone left, I sat in silence for a time, composing my thoughts, recognizing that what I had lived through would take ages, if not forever, to fully understand.

The memory of this experience wells up many times, especially when I drive past the hospital. I expect in the months to come, perhaps for the rest of my life, to unearth its treasure, for this event, more than any other, reshaped my life.

There are less traumatic times when we feel the need to be alone in meditation, to leave conversation behind us for a while. Communication survives as honest and compassionate exchange, thanks to these spaces of healing silence. There are many occasions when talk hurts, or we say too much. That's when we most need time to think. We value meditation because it gives us inner space in which to assess our words, to retract, at least mentally, what is hurtful, to release what may be of help.

Countless are the breakfast-table arguments that result in a sharp-tongued barrage of insults, followed by sullen silence. Husband and wife separate, each driving off in his or her own car, feeling angry, forsaken, verbally abused. It is possible that during their drive, while they are apart from one another, a reconciling meditation begins to occur. It is only a question of who will pick up the phone first to say, "Honey, I'm sorry. I guess I got up on the wrong side of the bed this morning."

A single mother told me how much she needs moments to meditate in the morning after her children go off to school and she begins to get ready for work. The noisy chorus of banging bathroom doors, loud gargles, crackle-and-pop cereal, backfiring motorcycles, slamming screens finally stills. She delights in the meditative silence that restores her spirits, in the quiet drive to her office and the temporary escape it offers from demands and distractions.

Meditation is enhanced by listening with one's inner ear finely attuned to spiritual meanings. On the drive home from the hospital, I heard on the radio the strains of a favorite symphony. Victor, at my request, turned up the sound. I had listened to this piece many times before, but never had I understood it so keenly. It was as if I had crossed in person the spiritual mountains and valleys described in the composer's score.

The music, combined with my own meditations on the heights and the depths, touched me to the core of my being. This whole experience enabled me to bore below surface meanings to mine life's harshest, most challenging mysteries. Tennessee Williams concluded in his *Memoirs:* "After all, high station in life is earned by the gallantry with which appalling experiences are survived with grace."

When I finally found the words to describe my state of mind to the people who care most about me, I was able to review what had happened with some degree of grace, to absorb and answer their questions as honestly as I could. I gave up trying to compose superficial explanations and spoke from my heart. To fathom all the repercussions of such a formative event was impossible, but at least one could raise the mystery to the light of prayer and ask for the gift of God's peace.

Meditation on major or minor events thus helps us to sort out thoughts as yet unformed or those disordered by the hectic nature of our day. Victor used to tell me that the best remedy he could find to clear his head was a ride alone on some country trail on his motorcycle or in his Blazer. We've all had similar experiences. One I'll never forget happened during and after a dinner party.

I knew the hostess fairly well, but I had to be introduced to most of the guests. We were to eat at seven, but, since everyone seemed more interested in drinking, the hour was pushed back to eight. In the meantime I was starving, having skipped lunch because of the occasion.

The level of conversation degenerated with each drink. I began wondering what I was doing there. The emptiness of cocktail chatter always depresses me. I did my best to appear animated, witty, but my face began to stiffen. I felt as if the smile I had pasted on would crack and fall off. Luckily, our hostess announced fairly early that dinner was served.

The people she placed on either side of me really wanted to talk to each other, so I became the net over which they passed their remarks. My thoughts raced this way and that. I tried to interject a few ideas, but they seemed to cause a foul in the game already under way.

When at last dinner appeared, it tasted flat. I needed fresh air but had to wait until our hostess sailed in from the kitchen with a lavish dessert, which everyone ogled and ate. I did manage to skip the after-dinner drinks without looking impolite and escaped to the solitude of my car. As a haven from thoughtlessness, it never felt so good. I drank in the outside air with an eagerness matched only by the way I gulped the first sip of water after surgery.

I took the long way home so that I could organize my thoughts. I wanted to test my brain, so to speak, to see if it was still working after several hours of mindless banter. I didn't blame the others who were there. They seemed to be enjoying themselves. I was the one who was different. Nothing pleases me more than an evening of good conversation with friends who talk and laugh together in mutual love and warmth. I should have known from past experiences that evenings with those who have no interest whatsoever in reflection leave me drained. I thought things over and renewed an oft-made promise to myself that I would refrain from accepting such invitations if and when I could do so without hurting people's feelings or harming necessary business relations. It goes without saying that I would have been happier had I spent the evening reading or listening to music. By the time I pulled into the driveway of my apartment, I felt much better. My thoughts were together, and I could go to bed without stress.

Such experiences offer us the chance to reflect on the mystery of our ever-elusive, ever-confirmed, divine life direction, especially when we doubt ourselves, feel different from everyone else, or lose confidence in what we are called to accomplish, however limited a contribution it may be. As long as we take time to listen with integrity to the inner voice addressing us in our here-and-now situation, we need not fear. God will show us the way to carry on while remaining faithful to His call amid the opaqueness and ambiguity of the human condition.

When we remember all that the Lord had to endure by way of petty opposition and the ultimate violation of His person, we feel less alone and misunderstood. Meditation enhances our understanding of life. It teaches us to carry on in compassion.

CLOSING MEDITATION

Return now to your meditative stance. Sit quietly. Breathe in and out slowly, deeply. Close your eyes again and recall in a concrete way what the Lord has done for you, how He has revealed His love. Sink into the ocean of His mercy. Listen to His words speaking in your heart, in the events of your everyday life. After a while, read this prayer as if you hear Him saying personally to you:

> My dear child,
> I am with you always,
> No matter how small,
> How unworthy you feel.
> My grace is enough for you.
> Be present to my call
> With childlike faith.
> Never will I leave you
> Orphaned.

Never will I take my love
From you.
In me your troubled soul
Can rest.
With me all shall be well.
Through me
You shall accomplish great things
Even if they are unrecognized
By the world.
Every event contains
My word, a message
For your ears only.
Think about it,
Meditate upon it,
And meanings unknown
Before this moment
Will be revealed,
For what I conceal
From the worldly wise
I freely give to you,
My little child,
Dearest gift
Of Father's love.

2

Openings to Prayer

OPENING MEDITATION

❧

Wherever you are, stop for a moment. Whatever you are doing, pause and be present. Let your eyes roam slowly over your surroundings. Listen to familiar sounds. Inhale your favorite scent. Run your fingers along a smooth or rough surface. Make a piece of buttered toast and really taste it. Let your senses come alive to the beauty of the world. Resolve at least for today to become aware of the many openings to prayer provided by ordinary reality. How wondrous to taste warm coffee, to start the car, to walk, skip, be silent, speak. Everything we see, everyone we meet, can be a pointer to the mystery that surpasses us yet remains ever near. Become more sensitive to being in the Divine Presence, and every moment can be an avenue to meditation. Action can be rooted in contemplation.

❧

Active people who want to live a more contemplative life often become discouraged because it seems as if there is never enough time left in the day to read, meditate, pray, or be present to the Lord, no matter what happens or where one is. This is a real problem. Does the solution require the initiation of more rigorous disciplines? Or might it have something to do with using more wisely the unplanned free moments available to us?

These times come when we least expect them: waiting for a bus that is behind schedule; standing in a checkout line at the supermarket; taking a leisurely shower; getting the car filled with gas. Such opportunities to place ourselves in the presence of God occur more frequently than we might think. Now is the time to call to mind a favorite text, to reflect on God's will, to ask for His help.

The time required for dressing or driving to the office can be filled with either distractions or divine musings. Mother tells me that some of her best moments for meditation emerge when she is doing such routine tasks as preparing ingredients according to a tested recipe; putting away bags of groceries; raking the garden; washing the car. Without knowing it she seems to be following the ancient adage of the spiritual masters, who advise us that the present moment is a sacrament manifesting a hidden mystery. In it, if we are properly disposed to grace, we may find sacred meanings in what might otherwise remain mundane appearances.

This reminder of the richness of the ordinary prevents us from equating holiness with churches, shrines, retreats, or rituals only. Every person, event, or thing is potentially holy. A child, a Christmas play, a cradle—each is an epiphany of the forming mystery that sustains universe and world. The face of our beloved, the fresh buds on a barren winter tree, the refreshing waters of a woodland brook, the sleek splendor of a tall building—all can manifest a higher meaning. What appears in time can point to the eternal. Each moment lived in loving attention to the transcendent can serve as a reminder that the God who calls us from beyond is infinitely near.

Let me share a journal entry related to the importance of

remembering the mystery amid our here-and-now encounters.

What is this elusive "it" for which everyone is looking?

. . . it may mean anything from true love to the perfect turtle soup, but where is "it" to be found? The relationship that will not disappoint. The community that will celebrate each member's creativity. The parent who will love each child unconditionally. Where is "it"? The office staff that never makes a mistake. The faucet that is guaranteed not to leak. The new car without squeaks. Surely, we are inclined to conclude, wherever "it" is, it cannot be where we are here and now. It has to be someplace else, maybe with a guru in India, or with a husband who looks like a movie star. Maybe in a parish whose pastor would never reduce preaching to the utterance of pedestrian financial facts. We long to hear great philosophical statements, a poetic whirlpool of meaning that sets our hearts afire.

To find "it" would be like catching a star, climbing an unconquered mountain, being drawn up in ecstasy by a love that knows no limits. Where is "it"? Why is "it" so far away? Should I leave everything behind me, burn my bridges, break through dull routines, drop everything? What does it matter as long as I can find "it"? So goes the human heart, sailing away on wings of expectation, never suspecting that the "it" for which one longs is exactly where one is.

It is near, as near as that dear face across from us at the breakfast table, as close by as the worn sidewalk on which tired feet trudge home from work, as proximate as the neighborhood, the community, the family within which we live. And why shouldn't it be there? That "it" we long to encounter is raw, primitive, ordinary reality. It is the stuff of which everyday life is made. The squish of a ripe grape on a hot summer day. The taste of salt on one's tongue as one dives sweating hot into a wave. The brush of lips between two friends who know without speaking that their love will never end. It is there, in the smell of hot apple pie, in the taste of peppermint, in the touch of a baby's finger on callused hands, in the sound of a single bird outside one's window on a foggy morn, in the sight of sunset over a softly rolling hill.

The "it" we seek is never far away. We have simply un-learned the art of locating it in the ordinary. We are duped into thinking that life has to be spectacular when in truth it is quite simple. What could be more simple, yet more wonder-ful, than a first sip of steaming coffee on a frosty winter day, than being given a flower by someone whose love transcends words? These ordinary events are replete with meaning. In something as insignificant as a blade of grass there is a sur-plus of marvel. There is mystery unfathomed in the dullest museum.

The "it" we seek is elusive, yet it is eloquently evoked everywhere. The point to remember is this: *If* we cannot find "it" where we are, here and now, in this place, with this person, we will probably miss it altogether. We will be like the explorer who gave up everything to seek diamonds only to find when he was dying that the most valuable crystal was lodged in the heel of his shoe. If we take time to watch the seasons change, to see the grass grow, "it" will unroll in ecstasy, in a bright epiphany of meaning, at each seeker's feet.

To take time—that is the key to living life from a spiritual perspective. An odd free moment I have cultivated, in which to pause and remember who I am before the Lord, happens when the traffic signal changes from green to yel-low. I am learning to welcome this legally enforced pause as a call to relax in my seat, to look around and rejoice in nature, to utter a prayer of praise or thanksgiving. For a long time the opposite occurred. I would miss the spiritual opportunity of these moments and instead grip the wheel, tense up my foot to pump gas, and accelerate the second the light changed from red to green. Why? I could not push my car through the intersection. All my straining was to no avail. I had to wait.

Our behavior at the yellow light can tell us a lot about our spiritual well-, or not so well, being. The pushing posture may signify that despite our good intentions to slow down and center ourselves in the divine presence, we live predominantly in the fast lane. We don't walk, we run. Time controls us, we don't discipline it. We are so concentrated on planning the day, on getting everything done, that we miss these messengers of grace. We don't hear the inner voice calling us to relax, to let go, to let God be God in our life. Our whole body posture, tensed behind the wheel, ready to forge ahead, tells us something is wrong. Here is a free moment, one to three minutes depending on the traffic flow, when we have nothing to do but rest our body, quiet our mind, wait peacefully, and bring ourselves into the presence of God. The moment passes, and we do nothing with it, whereas even attending to five of these pauses in the course of a twenty-four-hour period could add up to a fifteen-minute meditation.

These moments, combined with the other chances sprinkled throughout our day to pause and pray, could provide in total the hour we've promised to give to God. On the days we can give Him that holy hour all at once, everything is fine. But for the most part it may have to be spaced out, and what better way to start living in His presence than to stop, really stop, when the light turns yellow. In that "holy minute," present to the Lord, we attune ourselves to the pulse and pace of grace. We don't push beyond where grace wants us to go. To illustrate this point, let me relate a story told to me by a missionary priest.

"When I was young," he said, "caught up in the fervor of my future work of saving souls, I refused to listen to the warnings inside me. I dismissed haughtily my real fears and misgivings. I would be the kind of missionary who became a legend in his own time. No obstacle would deter me. Of course, I prayed that the Lord would use me to execute the great plans He seemed to have planted in my heart.

"A request came for missionaries in the then Belgian Congo. Yes, that's where I would go. I felt flushed with zeal, confident that I could overcome all obstacles. I rushed to volunteer as fast as my legs could carry me. The faster I went, the easier it was to forget my fears. I could more readily repress my secret hunger for music, poetry, and a gentle style of living. The latter was hardly in keeping with the rough-and-ready model of the missionary I had built up in my fantasy life. I would push these 'sissy' desires behind me and become a 'clean slate' upon which the Lord could write His will.

"So off I went, loaded with gifts from my family, to make my mark in the Congo. Nothing or no one could have prepared me for what I had to face, nor could I have anticipated such humiliating failure.

"The first sign that something was wrong occurred the day I had to drive to a remote outstation to take over the duties of a sick friend. I felt rather nauseous, but in typical 'tough guy' fashion pretended it was nothing. I told myself that if I could learn the local language, as I had done in a relatively short time, I could do anything. I pushed aside a gnawing anxiety, labeled it ridiculous, and got into the Land Rover. I started the engine, pressed the gas pedal, and almost passed out from a wave of weakness that surged from my toes to my thighs. I got out of the vehicle, thinking that if perhaps I took some tea I could make it in time. No sooner had my feet touched the ground than my knees buckled and I fell over. I couldn't even walk! I had to crawl on hands and knees back to my cabin, by this time arousing the attention of a boy who helped to take care of my chapel and grounds. He helped me into bed and under my instructions made contact with a nursing sister in the region. She came as quickly as possible, but was baffled by my symptoms, for my feet, my knees, my entire two legs were becoming stiffer and stiffer. In the end I had to be carried out and transported to the hospital serving our area. I was examined thoroughly, but no one in that particular clinic could discover the cause of my strange illness or suggest a cure.

"Eventually I was transferred to a special hospital for the treatment of tropical diseases in Belgium. Again neither cause nor cure could be found. Finally I faced the fact that I had to undergo in-depth psychotherapy. It was under hypnosis that I gained the insight and courage to admit that I was literally scared stiff by the demands of missionary work in the Congo. I had ignored the need to analyze where my real gifts resided, what they were, and how I could use them for the Church. Under the influence of what was fashionable and undoubtedly the right avenue of service for some, I had opted to adopt a posture of erratic heroism. I had definitely pushed myself beyond the pace of grace. Little wonder I collapsed and lost my peace of heart and mind. I have a lot more interior searching to accomplish. Actually I hope someday to be able to return to my mission, but this time with an open acceptance of my limitations. I know God can use me, but only if I don't misinterpret my own self."

After such an experience, this priest would probably understand the wisdom of pausing at, rather than racing through, the yellow light. A related incident comes to mind. It occurred in the sixties, when religious from a number of congregations were moving from suburban schools to apostolates in the inner city. After careful appraisal of their calling and talents, four brothers received permission to establish a new community in an apartment in the inner city, where they would also teach and do social work. A fifth brother, denying the intuition that such a harsh life would be unsuitable for him both physically and emotionally, gave way to the convincing propaganda that real service for the Church meant one thing: going to the slums. He asked permission to join the other four. Like them he wanted to live in such a way that nothing was too much. If they were strong enough to do social work and teach for eight hours, come home, grab a fast bite, and head out again to lead a rally against unscrupulous landlords, then so was he.

One look would tell anyone that he was much more frail than the other four, but, because he felt guilty about staying behind, he pushed himself to keep up with their expectations. He felt horrible if he shirked any responsibility. Before long he fell into the detrimental pattern of ignoring fatigue, repressing resentment and anger, always smiling, putting off prayer for a more quiet time.

The work to be done became the epicenter of his life. One evening the dreadful thing he was doing to himself became clear. He knew that he had reached the end of his rope and that to push himself any more harshly would most likely result in the loss of his vocation. Like his brothers, he had been working all day long with the chronically unemployed and their families. No sooner had the group of them sat at table to down their hastily prepared supper, than one of the four, a particularly robust fellow, spoke up excitedly. He had planned to be home that evening, but he felt that for the sake of justice, mercy, and peace all of them should go to a neighborhood meeting and join in the demonstration to protest a decrease in unemployment compensation. It occurred to the brother in question that for the sake of the same justice, peace, and mercy all he wanted to do was go to bed. The truth of his exhausted body struggled to be heard above the din of his exalted social ideals and the guilt feelings that had dominated his life so far.

For the first time he felt courageous enough to say no. Why deny who he was and what he had to do in the situation? He had all but lost patience with his limits. It was time to relearn the art of being compassionate toward himself as well as caring for others. Gently and gradually his self-confidence was restored. When false guilt feelings threatened to unglue him, he would handle them by listening humbly to the truth of his own bodily, functional, spiritual being—his truth as distinct from the graces and talents given to others more heroic than he.

The gift of presence helps us to be faithful to who we are in the situations in which we live and labor. It is at once simple and spontaneous, profound and practical. Placing ourselves before God becomes a buffer against negativity, hopelessness, inertia, and fear. Presence grants peace in the face of frustrations and hostility, envy and distrust. It restores compassion and joy.

The grace of presence enables us to disentangle ourselves from introspective self-scrutiny and preoccupation with imperfection. We know that, though we are sinners, we can place ourselves in the light of the saving love and glory of the risen Lord. Such faithful presence enables us to engage in tasks with competence and dedication, not sidestepping responsibility but working to incarnate Christian values to our fullest capacity.

The practice of presence unveils the eternal wisdom of God in the everydayness of the world as well as a wisdom about ourselves. It helps us to disclose a style of living in which we are relatively free of useless, energy-sapping agitation, anxiety, and tension. We know more assuredly where we are going. We find ourselves thinking, feeling, perceiving, and acting more in tune with our divine destiny. Life becomes less dissonant as we follow God's direction and begin to develop our graced potential for contemplative presence.

CLOSING MEDITATION

Lift your eyes now from the page you are reading. Focus on some point in your room, a candle, a painting, until you begin to feel peaceful. Do nothing. Simply be there. Inhale and lift this entire moment to God. Exhale and let go of your anxieties and fears. In your mind's eye, go through the object focused on to the mystery behind all things, yourself included. Sense in the stillness how God sustains you. Let yourself be carried by Him. Feel His divine energy flowing into every fiber of your being. Relish this occasion of consonance, you and God, sounding together. See Him beckoning to you, hear Him saying:

> Come with me and find
> The lost treasure of time.
> Amid the rush
> Of daily animation,
> Listen to a friendly voice,
> Play with a child's toy,
> Console those crushed by pain,
> Labor but not under pressure.
> Be present to birds and flowers,
> To meditation, music, and good meals.
> Take time to be silent, alone,
> Gently at home with my mystery.
> Time can be tyrannous
> If you let it possess you,
> Touching,
> If you let it caress you
> With memories of pure moments
> Spent together in patience,

In unpretentious situations.
Let us wait for one another,
I, the Shepherd, returning you
Steadily to the simplicity of heart
That marks one planted
In the sweet meadow of my presence.
Heed always this promise:
Remain in me,
And I shall be in you,
Filling to the full
The empty spaces
That await these tender graces.

3
Living Harmoniously

OPENING MEDITATION

To prepare for this reading, take time to center yourself. Repeat, if it helps, a favorite text like "I am with you always," "Be still and know that I am God," or "I am the vine, you are the branches." Repeat this text until you feel quiet within, until the tensions of the day start to subside, and you remember who you most deeply are: a person made in the form and likeness of God. Slowly, in an attitude of gentle compassion, become aware of whatever it is that prevents you from living more harmoniously. Do you distrust God's designs for your life? Are you pushing yourself too harshly or falling into patterns of laziness? Do you feel anxious without knowing why? Are you having problems with someone you love, someone you've hurt? Allow whatever disrupts you to come to the surface of consciousness. Observe its hold over you, the way in which it makes you less free, less joyful. Now take this disruption and turn it over to God. Let Him show you His plan, teach you the way, remove the fear, heal the hurt. Ask Him to help you integrate what you do with who you are.

The question is: Can one be open to the sacred and at the same time live in the midst of a secular world? Can one really be a contemplative and an active person at the same time? The obstacles to integrating spirituality and functionality seem insurmountable. I understand these voiced doubts and misgivings, for I personally wonder if it is possible to foster harmonious living in a fast-paced, demanding world. Unfortunately, everyday existence reinforces—it does not diminish—this either-or mentality.

Freeways promote the human passion to be on the move, while billboards proclaim the slogan: SLOW DOWN AND LIVE. Driving on the highway compels us to cross over into the passing lane, while scenic viewpoints remind us to loiter. A subtle dualism dictates the pattern of daily living: work-pray; tense up-relax; run-walk. Time controls us. The rule of thumb is: Don't waste a minute of it; don't meditate; don't miss any chance for success. Extreme postures predominate: pressure versus apathy; action versus contemplation; motion versus stillness. Opting for activity, we ignore headaches, ulcers, heart palpitations. We take aspirins and keep on pushing.

Must this conflict continue? Are we condemned to flip from one extreme to the other? Can contemplative dwelling enhance, or must it detract from, active doing? Once this exhausting pattern is interiorized, it may be too late to change it. Our task in ongoing formation is to get in touch with these obstacles before they take over. What, in fact, happens to productivity when we give some priority to contemplation?

Compare what occurs when we drive off the freeway onto a sleepy country road. We reach our destination, perhaps a few minutes later, but much more relaxed. We've enjoyed the scenery, stopped for a lemonade, stretched our legs. In similar fashion, contemplation complements action. When we take time for spiritual deepening, as when we slip into a slower traffic pattern, we actually increase our efficiency in the long run, to say nothing of the overall quality of our life.

This rhythm of dwelling and doing can and does affect our entire system. Generally, we feel less pressured, more aware of time as a peaceful flow rather than as a demanding tyrant. This approach marks the beginning of a more consonant lifestyle, as was the case with a parish priest who came to our Institute for a refresher course in spirituality. To appreciate the radical change that took place in his life, one has to realize that by the time he was forty his reputation for apostolic activity was legendary.

"You name it and I did it," he said. "Everything: cooking, hearing confessions, maintenance work, pastoral counseling. . . . It was impossible for me to say no to anyone, even when my stomach ulcers were acting up. In due time, I began to lose touch with the spiritual motivation, the deepest why, of my ministry. I kept thinking, now is the time to slow down, to practice the priority of prayer I teach. I need to get away for a while, take a sabbatical, do something for myself for a change.

"It was as if I became two persons: one, the outer me, working tirelessly for the good of others, satisfying my 'savior complex'; the other, the inner me, pleading not to forget my own physical and spiritual needs. Guess which side won. I fell into the trap of thinking I was a superpriest who could get along without being cared for either by the people or by the Lord. The crash was inevitable. I was playing with fire by playing God. How long could I expect to maintain the delusion that what I called humble service was in reality sheer pride?

"One day I took a good look in the mirror. What a tired face and thinning body! I wasn't exercising or eating right. All I did was to attack a mounting pile of morning, afternoon, and evening appointments. I kept on giving without taking time off to be restored. Now the neglect was catching up with me. Fatigue lines were etched around my lips. Every time I tried to slow down, to do some reading, to go to a movie, to have coffee with a friend, a little button flicked on inside, pushing me to respond under pressure rather than to be gently present to the limited person I was. I saw in the mirror the face of a man who was spiritualizing this proud stance by saying, in effect, that I had to carry much of God's kingdom on my shoulders. The results were ludicrous. Instead of meeting a gentle Christlike priest who radiated Jesus' own peace and joy, people saw me as a nervous, irritable person, whose anger and agitation seeped out at unexpected moments.

"This pattern of overexertion persisted for several months. Fortunately, a friend I trust convinced me to seek spiritual direction. Gradually I began to see that my need to master every situation, my inability to delegate parish duties to other people, my excessive striving for perfection—all of these behavioral patterns stemmed from my tendency toward self-exaltation. I even had to prove myself to myself. I couldn't relax and be just plain me. The proof of this showed up, interestingly enough, in my inability to go on vacation. Even when I was away I would be living mentally at my desk back home, remembering that it was piled high with work or anticipating what I had to do the minute I returned. Instead of relaxing, I would compete with myself to get in as much golf as possible, as much sun, as much sightseeing. I would fall into my hotel bed in the same exhausted state as I fell into bed at home.

"After several sessions with my director, I went away for one week in August. That was when this extraordinary experience occurred. I learned firsthand what it meant to care for others, to care for myself, to be cared for by God.

"Packing my car, I felt the nervous tension creeping up, but at least I was more in touch with what was happening. I drove slowly to my destination on Cape Cod, allowing my mind to drift back to the months of June and July. I had fallen into the familiar patterns of pressure and control. In addition to my regular duties, I had volunteered for several extra ones. But then, I always liked the laudatory remarks I heard about being a caring person. I tried to shrug off the tension, mainly by listening to what my body was telling me. The warning signs were there: nervous stomach, indigestion, trembling hands, sweaty temples—a far cry from the relaxed, gracious person I wanted to be.

"I realized I would lose my peace and fall into the same trap as I had before if I didn't cease introspecting. That's when I decided to go to the Cape. One day, sitting on the beach, I noticed that the tension was at last flowing out of my body. Tasks done and undone receded into the background. I was simply abiding in the present moment and enjoying it immensely. What were my accomplishments compared to the care God lavished on the world? A feeling unlike anything I could put into words began to invade my soul, a deeply religious experience. In breathless wonder I beheld—as with the eyes of a child—ocean, sun, sand, waves, my own body, in their transcendent beauty.

"Think of it. This earth, this cosmos, this small figure lying on the beach—so finely knit together, held, sustained, carried, created by the Lord's caring hand. Tears sprang to my eyes in the realization that I, this overworked, unworthy, limited priest, was infinitely loved. There was nothing to prove. It was enough to listen to that inner voice saying, 'You are my child. I care for you. I cradle you in my arms. I love you. I forgive you.'

"A sand crab scurried under my feet. I reached out so it could crawl into the palm of my hand, held it for a moment, then let it slip through my fingers to freedom. It was as fragile, as vulnerable, as dependent as I. If I felt such care for this tiny crab, how much more must God care for me. Slowly the feeling of wonder faded, only to be replaced by a

sensation of overwhelming tenderness. It was as if my whole
being ebbed and flowed with the undulating waves. The unspeakable order of everything in the universe spoke to my
heart and assured me of my place in this holy composition.

"From that moment onward, I could honestly say that
my life fell into a more consonant pattern of striving and
stilling, of attachment and detachment, of seriousness and
humor. I realized that being cared for by God and becoming
a caring presence to oneself were as important as genuinely
caring for others."

Why is it so hard for us to accept that God loves us as we
are with our limits and strengths? How can we grow to be
gentle—to avoid a harsh, judgmental response to our failings? A perfectionistic effort to be in control of every detail
of life closes us to the surprises of God. By contrast, gentleness prompts us to pay attention to our tiredness. We work
as energetically as we can without blocking out the body's
signals that it is time to rest. We cease pretending that we
are omnipotent and seek another's help. Because we have
learned to be compassionate toward ourselves, we can em-
pathize with the vulnerability of others. We can respond to
their needs without trying to play God.

One concrete fruit in this priest's life, evidence of inner
transformation, showed up in the quality of his sermons. He
noticed that they seemed to move people more. Prior to his
Cape Cod experience, he was dominated by performance
anxiety. His compulsive need for perfection prompted him
to talk above the parishioners. He tried to impress them
with his knowledge of theology or his concern for current
issues. Now he felt more able to be with them, not as an
expert with the answers but as a servant, as a fellow seeker.
Open to God in prayer, he tried to feel what they were
feeling. He thought of himself as a channel through which
the Lord could touch souls in need of spiritual inspiration.
His capacity to be a pathway for the Word depended on his

own depth of presence. In short, he could not give what he himself did not live. His words would remain mere definitions or abstractions unless they were rooted in personal religious experience.

Complementing his patterns of activity were spiritual practices like silence, formative reading, meditation, and contemplative prayer. Rather than being caught up in the immediacy of this or that demand, he would pause before acting to tune into the movement of the Spirit, to listen to the voice of his Divine Master.

If we are to remember who we most deeply are and to retain the gift of God's peace in our hearts, we need, like this priest, to foster stepping-aside moments—times, so to speak, when we leave the freeway for the farmer's road, times in which to reflect again on enduring truths and values.

Such was the desire of the poet Walt Whitman, who describes in his *Leaves of Grass* what happened to him during an academic conference on the topic of astronomy:

> When I heard the learn'd astronomer,
> When the proofs, the figures, were ranged in columns
>   before me,
> When I was shown the charts and diagrams, to add,
>   divide, and measure them,
> When I sitting heard the astronomer where he lectured
>   with much applause in the lecture-room,
> How soon unaccountable I became tired and sick,
> Till rising and gliding out I wander'd off by myself,
> In the mystical moist night-air, and from time to time,
> Look'd up in perfect silence at the stars.

The poet wants to keep the child in him alive. He does not want charts and diagrams to separate him from the awesome experience of the stars. How different his attitude is from that of the boss in Nikos Kazantzakis's novel *Zorba the Greek.* The boss personifies the calculative approach in contrast to Zorba's childlike wonder. One day, while out walking, he notices a cocoon in the bark of a tree from which a butterfly is about to emerge. He decides to hasten the process of this miracle of metamorphosis by blowing his hot breath on it. As planned, the butterfly comes forth before his eyes, but its wings are so shriveled that, after a brief flutter, it expires. He feels like a murderer and weeps with remorse. He knows without question that he must change the arrogant thrust of his life or risk losing the Zorba that resides in him and in each of us.

While we may know and trust the call to find a balance in our lives between dwelling with the Lord and doing what He asks (the Mary/Martha paradigm central to Christian spirituality), we easily err on one side or the other, falling from floating piety to plodding activity. Our life becomes an either-or proposition, as if awareness of the transcendent must be cut off from functional achievement, as if bodily pleasure must never be associated with prayerful presence, as if inspiration excludes incarnation. Nothing could be further from the truth.

Christians struggle continually to overcome these dualistic tendencies, looking always to the Lord in whom the human and the divine are inseparably united. We must be patient, for such progress in spirituality is not ours to command overnight. It takes a lifetime of trying, in tune with grace, to reclaim the mystery of our being made in the form and likeness of God—at once stretching for the stars and standing upon the earth. Despite our desire for integration, we forget the rhythm of labor and letting go, as this true story will testify.

Exhausted from several days of travel in South Africa, following a full schedule of demanding speaking engagements, I was delighted when friends said it was time to slow down and enjoy the natural beauty of the eastern Transvaal, especially the Blyde River Canyon and Kruger National Park. There was no need to persuade me how badly I could use a break. I had been moving so fast that there had been no time to absorb what I was seeing. My inner resources were running low, and a silent radar inside signaled me that it was time to restore quiet. My friends and I drove to the canyon in cheerful, talkative togetherness, watching the dramatic countryside unroll before us. Though one friend who lived in the region had been to our destination before, he could not have described its incredible splendor. One had to see it in person. We parked several yards from the ridge and began walking toward it. One felt this to be a place of sacred mystery, holding in hushed beauty the spirit of Africa. Never in my life had I experienced such still yet moving silence. It penetrated to the core of my being, evoking awe, gratitude, adoration. A thousand pairs of eyes could not contain the wonder of this place. It sharpened every sense. Crisp breezes brushed across my face, cooled my disquiet, and drew me to prayer.

No one spoke. Words would have been superfluous. They would have cracked the canopy of solitude that bound us mysteriously together. There was nothing to say or to do. It was enough to be present to the Divine Presence that dwelled in these untamed labyrinths of stone. I experienced a moment of sheer marvel standing at the edge of the canyon. Its majesty gave me back to myself.

Time passed as three friends lost themselves in the glory of God. The wildness of the canyon enabled us to reclaim our overworked selves. The minutes spent in its restorative silence refreshed our spirits. For the first time in many days, worries faded. Nature worked its magic and once again enabled us to be present to life as mystery. It was hard to break away from the canyon, so freely did it invade and bless the beholder. But the day was still young and the

Transvaal had more treasures to show us, this time at the Kruger.

For city dwellers, unaccustomed to seeing wildlife outside a zoo, it is hard to describe the sensation of viewing within touching distance a herd of gazelles or two giraffes crossing the road. Perhaps it was beginners' luck, but the animals appeared one after the other to our wondrous gaze: zebras, buffalo, lions, but, alas, no elephants. Where were they hiding? They certainly were not along the main road. Later in the afternoon, in a spirit of high adventure, convinced of God's care for innocent creatures, we turned from the paved trail onto an unmarked path. We were really in the wilderness, on a way unknown, but it was here that we found unmistakable evidence of elephants. As darkness descended, we discovered more and more droppings! The road became rocky and dangerous, but the presence of elephants was more manifest. Suddenly a huge python slithered along the side of the road. Baboons screeched an eerie warning, and the suspense was overwhelming.

We turned a sharp corner, rattled slowly over a dry riverbed, and, at last, our faith was rewarded. There we were in a small Ford, three friends, surrounded by a herd of wild elephants. They were as surprised to see us as we were to see them. We eyed one another in awed silence before the bull elephant bellowed his authority. The peal of that high-pitched, thunderous roar was as thrilling as the silence it was set against. It took wild elephants to tap the heart of the primitive that slumbers beneath our civilized exterior. Here was the Africa one hopes to experience—this land innately, superabundantly spiritual, that in one glorious day of driving cleansed our exhaustion and through nature's power restored our potential for transcendence.

CLOSING MEDITATION

God gives us the beauty of oceans, stars, mountains, and fields to refresh our spirits. To accept this gift, you don't even have to leave your room. To contemplate nature, just close your eyes and imagine yourself in a favorite place by the sea, or along a country road, or under a budding tree. Pretend you are there alone, only you and God. Walk quietly, enjoy the air and the silence, the play of light and shadow on the water, the gravel, the leaves. Think of what it must have been like when Adam walked with God in the garden of paradise. Stretch, yawn, relax your whole body. Reach out and take God's hand. Let Him lead you into deep meditation on the bounteous gifts of creation. In this blessed encounter, all dissonance recedes. In humble gratitude, turn to God and present with me this plea for harmony:

> Spirit of wind and sky,
> Free soaring eagle,
> Silent tribute to the sacred,
> Bring rest to this weary body,
> Temper this controlling ego,
> Rushing to accomplish works
> Cut off from your words.
> Reunite in splendid union
> Prayer and production,
> Labor and leisure,
> Recollection and participation.
> Let the oneness I feel
> On canyon's edge
> Cascade through my being
> As rain drops from high places

To wet valley's desert spaces.
Teach me to be still,
Knowing that my purpose
Is to do your will.
Your light received
Radiates through me
To worlds dark with fear.
First let me live with you,
Then let me give you away
Day by day, until that moment
When my soul, on wings of dawn,
Flies home free, carried
By your hand through time
To eternity.

4
Lifted to Glory

❧

Place yourself in the presence of God and begin this exercise by focusing on His power, majesty, strength. He is rock, shield, protector, prince, mighty Lord. Now reverse the meditation. Picture Him buffeted, mocked, crowned with thorns, crucified, dead, buried. What a shocking contrast to behold. From omnipotence to nothingness, from power to utter poverty. Dwell on this mystery for a while, on this paradox of divine humiliation. Offer your weakness to Him, as He offered His for your sake to the Father. Surrender to God all that renders you weak, and let Him lift it into glory. Meditate on this scene of God's defeat by human standards and await the miracle of Easter morning. Death, where is your sting? Violence, where is your victory? For out of the tomb He rises triumphant. Behold the risen Lord, who turns our mourning into dancing, our self-gift into gain of glory.

❧

In an era that promotes *self*-actualization, *self*-image, *self*-esteem, *self*-help, we tend to resist rather than resonate with such Gospel-rooted directives as deny yourself, lose yourself, annihilate yourself. These phrases sound harsh, dehumanizing, groveling. Their meaning becomes clear only if we see that the self we are to lose is not our real self made in the image and likeness of God. This deepest form is the seat of our dignity. It is open to the light of Christ, but, since the Fall, it has been obscured by a counterfeit form, prone to sin and dominated by pride.

Therefore, to find our true self, the Christ form of our soul, we must lose our false self—the controlling ego, hesitant to acknowledge its dependence on a higher power, fearful of letting go and allowing God to lead us. Our true self is capable of a surrender that strengthens. Our false self clings to safety zones (powers, pleasures, possessions) that are self-exalting but ultimately unfulfilling. Only when this pride form is lost, that is to say, only when it ceases to be dominant, can we find our unique self in relation to the Lord.

In our quest for self-liberation, we must pass through the needle's eye of self- or ego-annihilation. This passage evokes great fear, for it means that at least momentarily we will feel as if we are dying, as did the disciples on the stormy Sea of Tiberias. They were terrified because they thought their boat was sinking. Wake up, Jesus, wake up! Save us! We are about to perish. Alas, he rebuked them, where was their faith? Fear prevented them from being open to the self-emptying flow of perfect love, which renounces personal gain and looks solely at the Beloved. This love alone can cast off the terror of ego-desperation. It can transform fear into loving adoration of the Source of life and being. Out of these depths of self-denial, we emerge fresh and free like Lazarus from the tomb. Liberated from pride's bondage, we can pursue our destiny in response to the divine initiative. Still, the tension between God's call and our reluctance to respond does not diminish easily, as this story indicates.

Under threatening thunderclouds, a pilgrim made his way to a famous shrine. Turning a corner, he suddenly lost his footing and plunged down the side of a ravine. A sturdy branch broke his fall. He clung to it for dear life, crying aloud, "Lord, Lord, help me! Spare me from the fate of this terrible fall." Miraculously, the heavens parted. A voice from on high assured him in answer to his prayer, "My Son, I am with you. Do not be afraid." The pilgrim was overjoyed. "Lord, what must I do to be saved?" "Simply let go." The pilgrim pondered this reply for a moment, and then asked, "Is anyone else up there?" A little of this person, fearful, not fully trusting, is in each of us. We are not yet convinced that the Lord will tend to our needs, as a mother protects and nurtures the child on her lap.

It is interesting to relate this paradox of giving up and gaining to the experience of losing one's way on the road. When I am not sure where I am going, I get nervous. I hug the wheel, scanning the streets for recognizable landmarks. I feel as if everyone is looking at me because my car seems to be out of control. Often, in my intensity, I go past the destination. I miss a turn. I have to stop and ask a service-station attendant to point me in the right direction. Frequently I am told that I passed the address a few minutes ago. After many such experiences of traveling to new places, I've discovered that it is best to assume before I start that I am going to get lost, that in fact I have to get lost if I'm ever going to find my way.

When I untense my body behind the wheel and let go of the expectation that I can locate the road the first time, I'm much better off. In a strange way, even though I may circle the same block twice, the road finds me. In going around a new neighborhood, I become familiar with my surroundings. Once I know the route, I do not easily forget it. When I assent to the risk of being out of control, life has a way of showing me the right direction and the best approach to travel there.

In the past, I would have a tendency to tough it out, to get good and lost before I would humble myself to ask for

help. This stiff-necked trait is also being tempered. I am not
so embarrassed to pull into a gas station, take out my map,
and ask, "Where am I?" What better time to ask for help
than when I've lost the way. Now is the time not to fake
strength but to acknowledge my vulnerability. To admit
that for all my cleverness I'm totally lost is to take the first
step toward being found.

Such was the way of sinners with the Lord. Unlike the
proud, self-righteous Pharisees, who thought they could
earn perfection on their own merits, the poor of spirit knew
they had missed the mark. They were like lost sheep who
under no circumstances could find their way home without
the help of a shepherd.

The same happens when we seek competent spiritual direction. Only when we can say, "I'm lost; help me," can we
be found. Any lessening of arrogance implies a gain in humility, which means, in the words of St. Teresa of Avila, to
walk in the truth of who we are. Now, when I'm lost on the
road and a passenger asks me where we are, I don't pretend
to have the answer. I move along, trusting that the way will
be found.

This experience can be compared to what the spiritual
masters call the "divine darkness," a phrase that points to
the ultimate incomprehensibility of God, to the mystery of
His ways with humankind. In this regard, what we must
lose or give up is any illusion that we can master the mystery. We find ourselves engaged in a game of hide-and-seek
with God. Each revelation of who He is in our lives gives
way to a new awareness of His hiddenness.

No amount of knowledge, no experience, however sub-
lime, is comparable to the unapproachable light in which
God dwells. In this realm one cannot reach Him by concepts alone. One best experiences Him through love. Since
the divine essence is hidden from our intellect, faith alone is
our guide. God is always more than what we can under-

stand, taste, feel, or imagine. One may even lose the ability
to speak in this loving encounter between the soul and God.
One stands before Him, our home and destination, in wordless adoration, in the darkness of not knowing, in the night
of faith. What matters now is not willful striving but a humble willingness to abandon ourselves to the God who saves.

Once in a while we meet a person who by the world's
standards seems to be abandoned by God. In reality he or
she has been found worthy to live an intense life of surrender and faith. I shall never forget my meeting with such a
woman.

No sooner had I arrived at the community for a weekend
conference than the sister in charge asked me to save some
time Sunday afternoon to meet the nun whom everyone
agreed was the treasure of the community. I assumed she
was referring to one of their renowned teachers or artists,
since the congregation staffed a prestigious college. I promised to leave some time free for our visit and went on with
my work.

The conference ended around two o'clock. Before I said
good-bye, Sister reminded me of my promise. I hesitated for
a moment, thinking how little energy I had left for an animated conversation, but, after all, a promise is a promise. I
wanted to ask Sister who this treasure could be, but she
seemed disinclined to give any details. I quelled my curiosity and followed where she led. I had expected to turn from
the Provincial House toward the main building of the college, but to my surprise we instead took an elevator upstairs
to what was obviously the infirmary.

The corridors smelled faintly of bandages and alcohol. I
took a deep breath, fearing for some reason that I was enter-
ing unknown territory. Sister had been rather secretive, and
by now we were walking into the dimmest corner of what
she identified as the terminal wing. She whispered where we

were, ending with the assurance that indeed I would be
meeting the treasure of the community.

To this day I thank God that she did not prepare me for
what I was to see. Softly she opened the door of a small
room at the end of the corridor. There, lying in a bed too
big for her frame, was the most fragile human being I had
ever seen. The skeletal structure shone through her translu-
cent white skin. Though I had never before been present to
such a phenomenon, I believe to this day that I beheld a
living saint whose radiant love set the room aglow. She
greeted me warmly and told me that she had prayed all
weekend that the conference would go well. Her work for
the past fifteen years, while this disease was devouring her,
was prayer. People came from miles around to give her their
intentions. Some visited her in person; others sent their peti-
tions by mail, but not one of them went unattended.
Though she could do nothing but lie in bed, she never
seemed to have enough time to beseech God on their behalf.

I felt so small in her presence, so unimportant. She was
living at once the ways of purgation, illumination, and
union. Now I knew what Sister meant by calling her the
treasure of the community. She had followed Christ to the
foot of the cross, had truly lost herself, and had been lifted
by Him to glory. She was a living temple of transcendent
love.

As stark as such self-denial may seem, it is exactly what
Jesus experienced. He offered himself in total surrender. His
whole being was turned into a sacrifice pleasing to God. He
invites us in turn to offer ourselves to the Father with our
talents and temperaments. He asks only that we strive to
surrender ourselves entirely to Him. Compromise is possible, of course. We can say we prefer God and go on pleasing
ourselves, or we can choose for love's sake to travel wherever the Lord leads. The journey will draw us away from
passing consolations and into a deeper kind of darkness.

Lost are the logical categories of understanding, the idle expectations, the strained affections that characterized our self-assured, secure, former selves. We feel so lost. What do we know? What should we remember? How can we love like this?

Gradually we give up our quest for facile answers and begin to live in faith. No matter what happens to us, we place our hope in the Lord. We learn to let go of self-centered attachments and surrender wholly to Him. Because this road seems so hard to follow, every so often we need a living witness, one who embodies here and now the promise of redemption, who trusts as does a child the workings of Holy Providence for our ultimate good.

Once a friend of mine, en route to the Far East, decided to stop in Hawaii at Molokai, the site of the leper colony and hospital founded by Father Damien. He received a cordial welcome from the staff and told them how touched he was by their compassionate care. Being a rather artistic person, my friend was especially sensitive to beauty, order, and aesthetic surroundings. The hospital itself was a tribute to the noble people who suffered there, victims of a disease that meant in many cases their removal from ordinary society.

The nurse who served as guide asked my friend if he cared to visit the ward of the worst cases. He did not have to go; there was no obligation, for many could not endure the sight of such debilitation. Yet the patients would be profoundly honored by his visit. He approached the ward hesitantly, aware of life's mystery, of how it brought one to the fine edge of knowing and not knowing. The ward was dimly illumined, but no shadow could shade the depth of human deprivation. How could God allow good people to suffer from such a pitiful condition?

My friend felt anger rising in his throat like a whiplash, but before he could resolve it, the rage was calmed by the strange peace that pervaded this place. Eyes smiled, stumps of fingers waved, bald heads nodded welcome. He had come to console, but he was being consoled. He had come to minister to them, but they were ministering to him.

The nurse had been silent up to now, for she had learned long ago the lessons he was being taught. She said that there was one special person she wanted him to meet. At the farthest end of the ward, huddled in a cushioned chair, was a Chinese woman—by common standards the ugliest, most deformed person he had ever seen. Her fingers and toes had been eaten away by the disease. Her nose had sunk into her face. It looked to him as if she lived in constant pain. All that seemed to be intact were teeth. Through them she strung her rosary beads. Her eyes radiated faith and compassion, as if she understood how hard it was for him to behold her. In a flash, the surface ugliness he had seen was swept away. With new vision he saw the beauty of her soul. It dispelled the ugliness of her body. To this day, he maintains, a leper was one of the most beautiful women he has ever known.

The depth of her faith defies understanding. Everything that constitutes a positive self-image—physical health, effective production, social success—had been stripped from her. She had lost it all. Yet what she had gained through openness to the transcendent inspires whoever meets her.

Back on the mainland my friend had lunch with a medical doctor who used to be on the staff of the hospital. He told him that when he went there he was an atheist. He expected what he saw to confirm his conviction that there was no God. In fact, the opposite happened. He attributed his conversion to a woman, one of the saddest cases, a Chinese leper whose faith smashed the facade of his atheism and opened his eyes to God.

Our meeting with divine darkness teaches us that human effort is not able to lead us closer to our goal. We must let go and make the leap of faith. Then we need not fear losing our way. We begin to grasp revelations that exceed human understanding. Faith is a gift that allows us to be friends with God, to encounter Him as a Person who blesses and accepts our inmost self. Faith is not wish fulfillment or the result of fear to face the abyss. It is an answer to that cry of terror in the midst of the night, to that soul-sinking feeling that life is too short, to that doubt if it is really worthwhile to go on in the face of so much pain.

Minutes tick by; years come and go. The endless cycle of rewards and disappointments, successes and failures, flows on. What lasts? I have no answer but faith. That dark gift beckons me on. It assures me that I am living already in the presence of what I so ardently desire. In the midnight moment, my soul is in total darkness. Faith is my only guide as I move on that border between life and death, between aloneness and union with God. I can do nothing but wait until He meets me in the darkness and illumines my way. Only when I feel utterly lost, reduced to nothing, can I be found.

Such darkness is a fearful experience. Though I do not feel God's nearness, I have to trust that from these depths He will lift me to new heights. Only when I am reduced to nothing, as Christ was on the cross, to the extreme of humility, is there wrought between my soul and God that union of lover and Beloved that marks the culminating point of our journey in this life. Because the Lord loves my poor, imperfect self, He demands of me no more than I can bear. He frees me from deceptive projects that boast of self-salvation. He purifies my heart of foolish pride. He grants me the grace to carry my cross without the need for continuous consolation.

In this light, we can see that affliction is not a curse but a blessing. Some time ago I received sad news in regard to a dear friend who had been the picture of health until she

contracted a highly contagious disease during a trip she
made with her husband to the South Pacific. The cure required many months of rest in and out of hospitals. When I
received word of my friend's illness, I wrote her a letter that
I include here, together with her answer, for this correspondence reveals again how loss can be gain from a spiritual
perspective.

To her I wrote:

"In the midst of suffering, at a time when we are at our
lowest physically, we can let our vulnerable, dependent,
nonutilitarian side emerge. We can say, 'Here I am, Lord,
not too efficient today, not managing everything so well, just
suffering and trying to make some sense out of what is happening.'

"When our bodies fail us in some way, we are brought to
the threshold of spiritual abandonment. At such moments
we can sort out better than ever the essential from the peripheral, the ultimate from the temporal. I think that in
affliction we come closer to God. I believe that if these
blessed times of sickness are lived to the full, without undue
fear of our temporality, life after that takes on a new glow.
Suffering can embitter us, but it can also make us more
tender, more compassionate. Because of this experience, we
seem to appreciate the tiny moments of life. I had a taste of
this feeling when I lay sick after surgery, drained from the
medication and loss of blood. Life is still good, I thought,
yet I have to let go and, in letting go, it becomes even better.
I am less grasping, less in need of proving something, of
being in control. To let go is to fall into the hands of God."

In reply she said:

"Never was I resentful or inclined to question why this
disease should have come to me. I looked upon it as an
adventure that would open new doors, afford fresh insight. I
was filled with gratitude for my magnificent surroundings.
Being ill brought me into a kind of communion with all

others who suffer physically. I felt grateful to God that my trial in comparison was so light. Because my days were filled with reading, making notes, digesting and assimilating new ideas, writing letters like this one, I had not a moment's depression, which is a regular symptom of this disease. But in spite of these good gifts, there was a tremendous gulf between the letting go I assumed I was doing and my strong, controlling ego.

"Though I kept my bones between the sheets for one month, I still managed to involve myself with unnecessary details of the household, worrying about all manner of things. My brother-in-law even dubbed my four-poster bed 'control center.' At least I learned how much I need the practice and daily commitment of letting go totally. I am slowly inching along in this strange yet thrilling approach, which keeps the fine line of body, ego, and spirit balanced. Each day I see more clearly the folly of my apparent control, of my deep reluctance to be my 'vulnerable, dependent, nonutilitarian self'—gentle yet firm."

When my friend got sick, especially because she was used to good health, she felt powerless. She was drawn to ponder as never before the mystery of affliction. Instead of becoming bitter and depressed when her sickness became worse, she accepted this setback as God's way of teaching her to lose herself in Him, to move from the pain of crucifixion to the joy of resurrection.

Just as it is easy to love a friend when our relationship is smooth, so it is easy to love God when He lavishes upon us good fortune and spiritual favors. But can we love Him with the same intensity when He appears to have abandoned us? When our most fervent prayers seemingly go unheard? When severe and, to our mind, undeserved sufferings are cast upon us? If we can truly accept these afflictions as blessings in disguise, as crosses Christ has already borne, our love will prove to be enduring. We shall pass the test of surrender that brings with it inner tranquillity and lasting peace.

In giving up our need to master the mystery, we will have gained the grace of wisdom, that knowledge of God and self that enables us to walk in the truth and not turn away. Obstacles then become aids in disguise as we listen anew to these divine directives: Deny yourself, take up your cross, follow Me. What we deny is the burden of pride we do not need. What we take up are the myriad events of daily life that mark the path of joy and sorrow, union and separation, health and illness—the entire human condition. We follow One who has lived through it all, whose life of surrender results in a remarkable coincidence of productivity and peace, a mission fulfilled, a cup emptied.

CLOSING MEDITATION

None of us have to look far to find a cross to carry. In every family there is some form of illness or addiction, a sudden, debilitating accident, a broken marriage—the list is endless. The cross is imprinted on our own life and on the lives of those we love. Lift this cross in all its searing detail to Christ. Don't seek an explanation for suffering. It remains a mystery. The only sensible thing about it is that God Himself came down to suffer with us. He understands everything we are going through. Let there pass between you and Him a silent exchange of compassionate love. No answers. No questions. Only the stark reality of what is. Place it all before Him, hiding nothing of your anger, frustration, fear. Listen to Him say, "It is I. Don't be afraid." Treasure these words in your heart. Meditate on them as you pray:

Spirit of my Lord,
Lift the veil that hides the truth
That giving up self is really gaining,
For of what worth is self-sufficiency
If it obscures the truth of your being
With me?

Spirit of my Lord,
Remove the gates that block grace
From leading my soul to silences so deep
That only your voice reaches ears
Made to hear these loving messages
To me.

Spirit of my Lord,
Gather my broken being into your arms,
Detach my heart from worldly desires,
Guide me into desert places
Refreshing as the endless traces of your mercy
In me.

5
Trusting Our Troubles

Troubles and trivial things are oft-neglected sources of meditation. Yet, if we wait to go to God with dramatic conversions or ecstatic highs in holiness, we might not go at all. The prayer of presence means first of all being present where we are and bringing that here-and-now reality to the Lord. So take the trifle (a letter received from a friend, a good meal, a car that starts on a cold morning, a picnic on the beach) and turn it into a prayer of thanksgiving. Take the trouble (a sprained ankle, an argument with your spouse, a faucet that refuses to be fixed) and turn it into a prayer of petition or praise, since things could always be worse! Let everyday life become a ground for trust rather than an occasion for complaint. Change your stance from depreciation to appreciation. See obstacles as opportunities in disguise. Have faith that if the Lord shuts one door He always opens another. In short, make life itself—in all its motions—your source of meditation. Become not only a person who says prayers but also one who lives them.

There are days in our lives when we regret getting out of bed in the morning. One I'll never forget. To begin with the toilet didn't flush properly. I froze in the shower because the hot-water tank was empty. The toast burned. The milk had turned sour. The coffee scalded my tongue. I had to scrape a layer of ice off the windshield of my car. And, to add insult to injury, when I passed another motorist on the road to make up for lost time, he cursed me and, in language impossible to repeat, informed me that my driver's license ought to be revoked forever. I was so upset I didn't see the red light and had to slam on the brakes, almost causing him to smack into me. The barrage of humiliating insults began again. I wanted to sink under the seat in sheer mortification. The negativity of his attitude toward me was as intense as the negativity I felt toward myself.

Through a series of troubles, unwilled by me, I was faced with at least three spiritual challenges: to forgive an enemy; to try not to blame myself for these mishaps; to dampen the invasive doubt that God didn't care.

Our day-by-day spirituality is linked to such trivial events and troubles. We do not have to ask for crosses. They appear everywhere. We do not even have the option most of the time of refusing to take them up. We are taken up by them. We find ourselves in situations that resist our best efforts to gain control. The morning remembered was one of them. Everything went wrong, no matter what I did. The question was: Could I make some sense out of what was happening? Were these troubles pointers to the truth that we are not in charge of what occurs? All we can do is find some meaning in what is given—and that meaning can be positive or negative. The choice depends on whether we live primarily in a posture of benevolent love, emanating from the Beyond to us, or in a stance of proud negativity, marked by a basically malevolent view of others and of God. On this choice rests our basic option: "Do we choose to abandon ourselves in trust to the mystery of formation or do we let ourselves feel abandoned in a meaningless formation process?", a question raised by Adrian van Kaam in his book *Fundamental Formation.*

Negativity is a powerful obstacle to trustful living. We feel violated when someone, even a stranger, takes a dislike to us for reasons unknown. It is as if we can do nothing to redeem ourselves in this person's eyes. We are the victim of his or her animosity. Such incidents are numbered among our heaviest crosses. We really feel hurt and are tempted to return insult for insult. Negativity, malicious gossip, the destruction of a reputation—these unspiritual attitudes have a harmful effect on our human and Christian formation.

It is sad to realize that we can become sources of emotional suffering in one another's lives. The pain multiplies when it is accompanied by pointing a finger and by an inability to forgive and forget, to let go of the hurt, to start over again in a healing relationship.

One of the worst things we can do to persons is to put them on a pedestal—as if they can do no wrong, as if they are not permitted to be human, which means, of course, to make occasional mistakes. Then, when they do reveal their human side, we tend to judge them harshly. What they did wittingly or unwittingly is blown utterly out of proportion, not at all in tune with the reality of this or that incident. Telling stories about how terrible they are only serves to arouse our pent-up rage and to enhance our obsessive analysis of their personality. This results at times in a violent outburst, which may devastate them. Under such circumstances, trust is difficult, if not impossible. Relationships may be scarred for life. The persons involved may be able to maintain surface civility, but deep-down feelings of trust are tragically lost.

I remember when I was in high school refusing to become part of a clique that formed around a teacher who played favorites. As a consequence, at a peak time of teenage vulnerability, I had to put up with second-rate parts in high school productions, a lack of popularity with the in crowd, an excessive concern over grades in the courses she taught. One encounter with this teacher, whose trust I never seemed to earn, still burns in my memory.

During rehearsal for our junior play, in which she had assigned me the role of a minister's housekeeper, I watched as she embarrassed to the point of tears another student, also not part of her clique. In his nervousness, he forgot the few lines he had to say, thus causing the lead actor, one of her pets, to miss his cue. The tongue-lashing this fellow received frightened me too. I was so relieved when, at the end of this vicious critique, she stamped her foot and bellowed, "Take five."

I found my fellow sufferer weeping backstage. I put my arm on his shoulders, and offered for what it was worth my feeling that his mistake did not warrant such a gross response. She must never have tasted the milk of human kindness. Ice water ran through her veins. She had a jealous heart made of stone. The words had hardly passed my lips when I looked up and saw her smirk. She was standing behind the curtain and had obviously heard everything. Our eyes met and a cold tremor passed from the tip of my head to the bottom of my toes. I felt as if the entire school year were ruined.

I went home and laid the dilemma before my mother. We talked things over and decided that indeed the teacher had been wrong to insult this boy. Even so, I was out of turn by talking so meanly about her to him. As a student with required courses under her at stake, I ought to offer an apology. I balked at the advice, but in the end swallowed my pride and found an opportune time to approach her. I can still recall her classroom at the end of the day, chalk dust settling on the windowsill, smells from the chemistry lab drifting in through the door, and she sitting alone behind her desk, bent over soon-to-be-graded midterm papers.

I felt as if my heart were banging as loud as the lockers being slammed shut by departing students. My palms began to sweat. I prayed to the Lord that I would not faint before this ordeal was over. I stood before her, cleared my throat, and waited. The moments were endless before she looked up. It was the first time our eyes had met since the event backstage. Hers had no more warmth in them now than they did then. The words I had rehearsed moved me to explain my response to the incident until I reached the point of official apology, saying, "Please forgive me for what I said about you. The words were spoken in anger, and I'm sorry if they hurt you."

What she said next still sends shock waves through my spine. "I forgive you, but under no circumstances shall I forget." My face may have registered disbelief, I don't know. All I know is that when she lowered her eyes silence fell from the ceiling of that room like dank leaves floating from dead trees through dense fog. The air felt that heavy. I knew I would pass out if I uttered one more word. I turned quickly and walked out the door. I ran through the empty hall, gasping one deep breath after another to regain my balance.

Looking back on this event, I realize now that it taught me more than any book could about the nature and meaning of negativity. I was not forgiven that day because the person to whom I apologized refused to forget. Because she could not let go of the offense, heal her feelings of negativity, put away the past, and start anew, forgiveness could not be wholeheartedly extended. The blame rested on me. I'm still left, in relation to her, with unfinished business. I passed her classes with good grades, but I never felt like a full person. She died a few years ago. I wonder if eternity's expansiveness has enabled her to forget the hurt and at last really forgive me.

We are fallible and weak. At times our actions are unwise, our motivations impure, but we need to avoid doing violence to one another by trusting that we can be open to the truth, that we are able to grow once we see it. It takes courage to operate on the basis of this kind of trust. It may mean facing a teacher with what appears to be favoritism or admonishing a friend about divulging privileged information. By the same token, building trust means that we have to be open to the suggestions and criticisms of others, willing to bear responsibility for our actions, especially when they prove to be wrong.

This ordinary human experience reminds us that interaction with the people and events that make up our daily world breeds ambiguity. There is no way out. What I consider a perfect piece of driving may cause the person behind me to shake his fist. To live is to be in conflict. It is to be faced with the challenge of choice. Burying feelings without any kind of insight or resolution only postpones or intensifies the issue. The answer is not to submerge the conflict under pious rationalizations but to appraise how and when one does bring it out in the open. *How* depends on one's personal sensitivity, on past experience, on insights and graces received in the actual situation. *When* depends on practical judgment of the most appropriate opportunity for a confrontation, a frank discussion, or a slight defusing of the tension in an atmosphere of kindliness and compassion.

Expression of conflict can have positive results if it flows from love and concern for the other. Traces of pettiness or hostility may signal that a slush fund of animosity is about to spill over. In that case, old accumulated anger may flare up and gush over, when all we wanted was to express disagreement. Conflict becomes a source of destruction rather than a sign of growth. Real communion occurs not when we resolve our differences, but when we remember that our life together, imperfect as it is, is a response to God's command to love one another as we love ourselves.

Not surprisingly, what destroys togetherness faster than anything is a spirit of negativity. Charity disappears when we feel obliged to put other people down. Tragic as it may be by human standards, some people seem to thrive on labeling others and keeping them in their place. The negative spirit diminishes both the person who harbors it and the one on whom it is vented. The driver who wants to push me off the road hurts himself as much as he hurts me. No wonder an encounter of this sort can put a damper on our entire day.

What of the person who brings a black cloud along wherever he or she goes? We were obliged on occasion to invite such a lady to our home. Depreciation, negativity, gloom, lack of trust flowed out of her entire system, creating around her dark vibrations that could spoil almost any gathering. She was the type of person who can make a hostess feel on edge days before a dinner party.

I'll never forget one such occasion. We cleaned the house twice, knowing from past experience that she could spot a speck of dust at a distance of two feet. Mother slaved to prepare a faultless meal, beginning with wedding soup, a delicious Italian specialty that takes a full day to cook.

Our guest arrived, perfectly dressed. A slight tension hung in the air, but that was to be expected. Much to our surprise the day was sunny; usually when she came it started to rain. Mother called us to dinner just as we had exhausted the last bit of small talk. It was clear that we had succeeded with Operation Dust, because her gloved finger, swiped slyly across the bookshelf, had emerged gleaming white. Maybe this good start would be enough to dispel the usual gloom.

Alas, our luck was on its last leg. We gathered around the

table, offered grace, mouths watering in anticipation of the savory soup. The table was set elegantly, the soup served graciously, the mood friendly and light. Our eyes automatically focused on our fussy guest to see if we had passed the next test. Suddenly, to our horror, she lifted her first spoon of soup out of the bowl and, as if the fates had foretold it, there, dangling from the steaming edge, was a sharp sliver of chicken bone. It occurred to me that if that bone had only found its way into my father's bowl, he would have tucked it silently under his plate to save my mother this embarrassment. We watched in perverse fascination as she picked the bone from the spoon with two manicured fingers, held it aloft for a solemn moment, and then transferred it, as if drying a wet twig on hot sand, to a bare spot on Mother's best beige tablecloth.

Nothing was said, but the rest of the dinner was ruined. Seeping through the dining room walls was the black shadow we thought for an innocent moment she had left behind. By the time dinner ended, for the most part in strained silence, as if on cue it began to rain.

What is it that sustains us under this pallor of negativity, this paucity of trust? We can bow under the weight of harsh criticism and begin to hate the source, but that only harms us. One has to feel sorry for this woman, for her attitude makes life in and around her joyless. I wonder if she ever has a truly generous, truly peaceful moment. God only knows what goes on in her convoluted fantasies of perfection and persecution, for she is convinced that the world is out to get her, that it is her responsibility to keep the whole dusty mess under tight control.

The negative energy she exudes eats away joy the way vultures pick at a carcass. As a result, people do avoid her after so many meetings. In the beginning she makes a fine impression. Her apparent form can be quite charming as she discusses the latest fashions or trends on the political scene.

She is articulate, witty, adept at dropping the correct compliment here and there to impress new friends. In due time her deadly sting surfaces. People who liked and trusted her feel the poison.

This woman became a vivid example of all that I would not like to be. No one makes a perfect grade in human relationships, but at least we can try to become more sensitive to the feelings of others. We can try to treat them courteously, not upsetting them unnecessarily by our words or behavior. We promise not to pinpoint their mistakes so as to read them back to them months later, nor do we put them on a pedestal and then condemn them when they fall off. It is as disrespectful to impose our convictions on others as it is to insist that they always do things our way. Rather, we ought to respect the unique gifts God gives each person, for one person's strengths may compensate for another's weaknesses.

To pour coffee in the morning, to be on time for a meal, to clean the house, to answer the telephone, to drive someone to the doctor—these ordinary endeavors can become avenues to trust in the basic goodness of God and others, if they are done with loving hearts and hands. Higher values need not be expressed in heroic ways, for the truly heroic is usually hidden in everyday routine. Life is made up of little things. We embody our highest aspirations in concrete moment-to-moment actions. Everyday life is the vessel that carries spiritual ideals. In small, unnoticed ways, the fullness of eternity enters the finiteness of the temporal. There we transcend what is petty, distrustful, and immature. There we become men and women of true prayer.

CLOSING MEDITATION

Morning dawns and with it comes the chance to make a fresh start. Our prayer life may have become lax but the Lord never loses patience. Each day He calls us anew to be carriers of His care and concern. Reflect, therefore, on what it is in your life that hinders the flow of His love. Are you irascible, judgmental, nagging? Work with His grace to remove these blockages. Be patient with yourself. Remember, you and I are immersed in an infinite sea of forgiveness. Pray for the vision to behold His face in every place of labor and leisure. Pray for the strength to maintain your pledge to be an epiphany of His love and tender mercy. Give thanks always and everywhere, praying with confidence:

> Lord Jesus,
> Though at times I betray
> Your presence, forget your promise,
> You tenderly entrust me
> With your word.
> Despite my weakness
> It whispers strongly in my soul.
> You are forgiveness itself,
> You are love and loyalty,
> Accepting me,
> Even when I turn away haughtily.
> Everlasting is your pledge
> Of fidelity.
> To trust you is to turn
> Trivial events and troubles
> Into occasions of transcendence.
> Create in me a humble heart,

Ready in peaceful obedience
To do what you will,
To fill with your graces
The empty spaces
That in you grow still.

6
Breaking Down, Breaking Through

త్

Loss of control, dashed expectations, betrayed trusts, break-downs of one sort or another—such crises test faith. We would prefer not to go through them, but what choice do we have? We have to carry on as does the captain who must steer his ship into the storm to find safe port or the pilot who must land a plane low on fuel. The deliverance promised on the other side gives them the courage they need to get past the danger. When we feel least ready, tough times come upon us. It's like living for years with a beautiful, admired, intact set of fine china. Suddenly one piece after another cracks and breaks. There are no replacements. We have to either live with a mismatched set or buy a new one. Have there not been times when your life was like that china set: perfectly to-gether and then bit by bit cast apart, dismantled by a series of resistances that tried your faith to the limit? The only advice that made any sense was to wait and see what God was doing while you sought a new direction. For this meditation, try to remember and perhaps record in your journal the turning point when light began to break through the darkness of not knowing what to do, where to go. When you saw, however dimly, the meaning of the mess to which you had been subjected. When harmony was gratuitously restored and you felt at peace with yourself and God. Keep this moment of grace in mind and you'll be less devastated by the next broken cup or chipped saucer.

⚜

Seldom, if ever, can we see the full meaning of events when we are in the middle of them. Only in due time, as we look back, do we understand what really happened and why. This retrospective glance is especially necessary during those periods when we fail, suffer, feel anxious or threatened in any way. Coping is especially difficult when we are under intense emotional strain. At such moments we need more than ever to trust in the benevolent direction of God's providence in our lives. We must be patient when things are at their worst. Then we can assign, with God's help, some meaning to what remains full of ambiguity to the untrained eye. Nothing can replace experience in this regard. If we have to choose between an apprentice and a master, we usually go with the latter.

For instance, my brother is an excellent mechanic. He has taken his car apart and put it together more times than I can count. Whenever a vehicle breaks down in the neighborhood, the owner calls him for an expert diagnosis. He opens the hood, checks the engine, tinkers with a few parts, tells the owner what is wrong, where to fix it, and how much it should cost. This is a great gift, one which particularly impresses me because, in relation to my car, I have only one wish: that it will take me to and from my destination intact. For this reason I trade it in every two or three years so that I can drive a fairly new vehicle. In theory this is a good plan, but in practice it doesn't work perfectly, for, like the human body itself, a car develops problems and needs to be repaired.

When I discovered my brakes going bad after a year of normal driving, I felt angry, frustrated, and compelled to campaign for quality of production, but then I began thinking, What am I so mad about? Everything breaks down, be it our best-laid plans, which inevitably go astray, or our bodies, which contract disease. I watched from my apartment window, which overlooks the city, as half of the buildings downtown were demolished to make way for several new skyscrapers. Forms fall and rise, break down and build up. Such is the fluid yet fixed dynamism of life, that strange blend of discarding and reclaiming, of dying and rising.

We are acutely aware of death and life when our own body, like an old machine, ceases to function well. Sickness puts us on the threshold of limit and possibility. We feel torn between our desire to keep on directing life and our awareness that it is no longer under our control. As we abandon ourselves to medical experts and pharmaceutical aids, we have no choice but to let go. As we let the reins of efficient functioning slip out of our hands, we may experience a release of creative powers and reflective capacities that were lying dormant inside us because we were too busy doing other things. In breaking down we break through to deeper levels of self-awareness in relation to time and eternity.

I remember how terrible I felt when my maternal grandmother died. I was only twelve years old at the time I had my first taste of the tragic separation death brings. Her body had failed her miserably as day by painful day she lost the bout with stomach cancer. Yet throughout her illness, as Mother nursed her, she taught us lessons of faith and courage not to be found in any book. When she finally died, an indescribable, aching emptiness was left where once the warmest person had been. It was as if the emptiness would

never pass, yet it did. Time healed the wound of her absence, and with that healing came a deeper sense of her
presence. The physical person was dead, but her spirit was
more alive than ever. All she stood for at the end had to
become in some way a part of my being—her humility and
humor, her dedication and endurance. What initially appeared to be a curse of fate turned out to be a blessed event.

This paradox of breaking down and breaking through
never ceases to amaze me. Once, when I was giving a talk, I
noticed in the audience the face of a woman whose eyes and
features I found both ethereal and enormously attentive.
She was soft and gentle, eager and receptive. It seemed as if
I were speaking only to her. At one point our glances
blended in confirmation of this affinity. Thus I was not surprised when after the lecture she asked if we could talk
privately. We walked to an adjacent parlor and sat face to
face. Before a word was exchanged between us, she became
misty-eyed. Had I offended her in some way? Far from it,
she assured me. It had been as if I were talking directly to
her. What she said next startled me because it was a rather
personal question. She asked me if I liked her face. I was
momentarily taken aback but answered honestly that I
found her to be a lovely person and was puzzled by her
concern. She wondered if I hadn't noticed how ugly and
pockmarked her complexion was. She personally felt her
face was repulsive.

The broken condition of her self-image shocked me. I
assured her that the quality of her skin had nothing to do
with my liking her face. So what if it was imperfect? It in no
way diminished her inner attractiveness to me. Had she ever
thought that perhaps the suffering she experienced because
of bad skin was what made her so receptive to the sufferings
of others? Could there not be some good in what she identified solely as a limit?

We shared for a while; then I asked her if she would do

me a favor the next morning when she arose and went to the
bathroom to wash her face. Would she find reflected in the
mirror her reddest pimple, touch it gently, and say, "I love
you, little blemish," for in being able to affirm her pimple
she would be able to love her limits, and in loving her limits
she would come to love herself, for these limits were the
gifts that made her unique.

Fear of failure is part of being alive. There is in us an
innate drive to right what is wrong, to perfect the im-
perfectible, to perceive limits as obstacles rather than opportunities. Yet each breakdown, whether of an object or of a
human body, can represent a new beginning. Death, we believe, is a transition to a fuller life. It is God's way of calling
us beyond ourselves. These crises of limits can give us wings
to reach new shores of hope and possibility.

When our pastor, a person deeply loved by the parishioners, was asked by the Bishop to leave the old neighborhood
and move to a new church many miles away, he could have
responded to the assignment angrily, obeying because he
had to. Instead he wrote this letter to all of us who love him:

> . . . if I had three months or three days to take leave of
> you, the bottom line remains the same. I cannot emotionally
> meet each of you without making the leave more painful than
> it already is. Please, I just cannot say good-bye to you. You
> have been my mother and father, my brother and sister . . .
> and so I can't as such take leave of you. I can only go,
> knowing that our love for each other will endure beyond the
> contents of this letter, and even beyond the Church itself.
>
> For heaven will be the perfection of our beautiful, loving
> relationship . . . that we have and will continue to have and
> will enjoy for eternity. I have always been yours and you
> have always been mine. I just want to leave it that way. I
> shall come home . . . and like family, we shall catch up on

all that has happened while we were apart and then, like family, it will seem as if we never separated.

You and I have been good for each other. I got the best out of you and you got the best out of me. What else counts?

I can never tell you how deeply I appreciated your giving me yourself so generously; you are truly special people to me.

Please . . . let us just go on . . . but always, my beloved Parishioners, always, let us treasure our bond of love.

This transcendent attitude in the face of limits reveals the human capacity to find meaning in apparent meaninglessness. The good times of peace, prosperity, and harmony are few and far between. When they happen, they are like pointers to that eternal home we believe awaits us at the end of our journey. More often than not, we live day by day through sickness, pain, loneliness, and disappointment—little deaths that make us aware of how little control we really exercise over our lives. Plans we thought were firm slip away, and we have to prepare ourselves for unexpected challenges.

One of these little deaths occurred in the life of a young priest I know who was writing his dissertation in Rome on a lesser-known Carthusian, a contemporary of the Rhineland mystics of the fifteenth century, by the name of John of Landsberg. This priest loved ferreting through old libraries, collecting data, organizing his card file, and constructing an outline for his writing acceptable to the theological faculty. The research energized him. Each day bore the fruit of a new fact, a nuance about the mystic's life not known before. One could not help but feel that he was a happy man, one who had found, at least for the moment, his purpose in life.

Thus, when he appeared one day in the classroom of the friend who told me this story, with pale cheeks, sunken eyes, a slight twitch around the lower lip, it was clear that something horrid had happened, like the death of his only living parent. Actually it turned out that he had received a letter from his Bishop in Canada, notifying him that he had been appointed spiritual director of the seminary and would have to return to assume the position in a few months. He could work on his dissertation in his spare time and during the summers, but for the moment his expertise was needed at home.

The priest held the letter in his trembling hand and appeared quite distraught, especially about one paragraph in which the Bishop confided that he was deeply concerned about certain sexual problems that were emerging among the seminarians. Of course, the letter meant that he would have to leave Rome, but that was not so upsetting. What terrified him was his own lack of preparation for such a task. His theological knowledge was fine, but what did it teach him practically about everyday formation in a seminary? Moreover, as much as he loved and learned from a superb mystic like John of Landsberg, the man to his knowledge had never written anything about the emotional and sexual problems that may erupt in seminarians today.

My friend tried to calm him down, but his fears were not to be dispelled on that fateful day. The letter from home had shattered his plans for his life. He felt overwhelmed by this assignment and could find some relief only in meditating on a favorite sentence from the Gospel of St. Luke: "You must stand ready, because the Son of Man is coming at an hour you do not expect" (Lk 12:40). He trusted that his fear of the unknown would decrease as his faith increased. He prayed for the grace to make the transition from the realm of theological speculation to the practicalities of priestly formation. For that task he would need to draw upon his study and life experience and daily to make an act of deep faith.

The winter of these breakdowns does give way to the spring of new beginnings. It is like the aging process in relation to the seasons of one's life. In our "summers," we experience exhilaration, openness, energy, the freedom to challenge and be challenged. In the "autumns," we suffer a loss or a stripping of vitality. In the "springs," we know the wholeness of growth in peace and joy, but before these times of new starts, there are the "winters" of defeat, struggle, suffering, unwanted change.

To the naked eye, winter seems bleak and dead, but in actuality growth is taking place in hiddenness beneath the soil, as plants prepare to thrust themselves freshly into spring. As in nature, so too in life we must believe that dark times provide the soil for deeper commitment. Then, in God's time, we too can say:

> . . . winter is past, the rains are over and gone. The flowers appear on the earth. The season of glad songs has come, the cooing of the turtledove is heard in our land. (Sg 2:11–12)

We do not choose such winters. They come upon us with all their heaviness. The only choice we can make is either to let go in faith or to become more frustrated. There is no way out; there is only a way through—the way of faith, of hope, of love. These winters kill our illusions of unlimited strength. Our world becomes more real. We are aware now of who we are, of what we can and cannot do. Especially in the beginning of a winter phase, we may feel a dull emptiness in the face of what we are not, of the things we have not done. It is exactly in this void that the fullness of faith, hope, and love can flow. In the words of St. Paul to the Corinthians:

> The trials that you have had to bear are no more than people normally have. You can trust God not to let you be tried beyond your strength, and with any trial he will give you a way out of it and the strength to bear it. (1 Cor 10:13)

Surrender to God and patient endurance are the way through the dryness and emptiness of this breakdown moment. The pain we undergo is a normal part of the crisis of limits. Going through it is not a matter of self-recrimination but of abandonment to Divine Providence. To give ourselves over to this experience in God is to believe with all our strength that his grace will be sufficient for us amid the trials we are suffering. A tunnel is dark, but there is always some light at the end of it.

CLOSING MEDITATION

As surely as we live, we shall lose our way. We are like children in a forest who know the general direction home but who end up taking a long detour. Be with those children in your meditation. The trees are thick. You cannot see the sun. There are many paths to choose, so you start walking. One way leads to a clearing. Another takes you deeper into the thicket. But you keep going. Picture the Lord waiting for you at home. He sends out signals to safety, even though you may not be able to see them. He is like a Shepherd who never sleeps until He gathers every stray in the flock. Recall when He has shown you how to turn detours into correct directions. Count the times when He has asked you to be patient, to quell your urge to find instant solutions to every problem. When we are lost—painful as the experience is—it usually teaches us to listen, to intercept the right messages, to call for help. In this attitude of faith and surrender, we are more likely to hear the Lord say:

> My little one,
> Remember my words:
> I will not leave you orphaned.

Why then do you worry so?
Outside me you meet
With endless disappointment.
Your furious pursuits
Of power and possession
Rob you of rest and gentleness.
Yet these breakdowns
Do not mean that I have
Left you forlorn, without consolation.
They are an invitation
To break through
To new heights of faithfulness,
Free of any selfish wish.
Learn from me
To take up the burden
Of this cross, this seeming failure.
In the mirror of my love
You shall see new meaning
Amid the fragments
Of human history.
Each scrap reflects
The eternal splendor
Of my mystery.
Behold the light I radiate
Even in the darkest place.
Let the living message
Of my gentle care
Quell your fears.
What need is there to worry
When my wounded hands
Hold you and all else
In the world?

7
Blessings in Disguise

OPENING MEDITATION

✧

As evening draws near, gather yourself together before God, bend back on the day that has passed, and begin to assess its blessings, however slight they may be. Think about these gifts in relation to every level of your being: physical, functional, spiritual. Be especially mindful of those moments when limits were revealed as signs of God's love—for example, the fatigue that led you to take a short nap, rising refreshed; the deadline that compelled you to stay at your desk, producing a good paper; the dryness in the depths of your soul that drew you to spontaneous prayer, giving way to undeserved consolation. Try to remember other times when you've felt God's hand guiding you through spiritual deserts. Picture Him as a God of many surprises with a divinely unpredictable sense of humor. In this meditation, concentrate on His nearness, on His motherly love for you, on His playful good nature. Centered in Him, forget your burdens and, for this brief moment, count your blessings.

✧

One by one, in the pale light of the basement church, people approach the communion rail to receive the Body of Christ.

Look at their faces, wide-eyed, wrinkled, rigid, relaxed. Not one of them, not even the most sophisticated of them, neither the woman in mink nor the emaciated bag lady, is without misery. They come to the altar for consolation and courage, in petition and praise. I watch in awe from the front pew of this inner-city chapel as the faithful file silently toward the Eucharist: slick corporation executives beside blue-collar workers; mothers caressing children beside coiffured career girls; teenagers with T-shirts proclaiming "Keep the peace" beside young upwardly mobile professionals. All seek mercy, even those whose posture, dress, and mannerisms seem free of misery. They, too, know suffering, hardship, pain. Their lot draws down the love of God.

How many parents here have lost children under tragic circumstances? How many men and women are divorced, separated, widowed? How many of those walking tall harbor a terminal disease? Who knows? All one can say for sure is that each of them shares in the general sorrow of humankind calling out for solace, forgiveness, gentleness. Why must the mercy of God be as tender as a mother's love and as severe as the executioner's cross? Why do we go on hoping in the midst of apparent hopelessness? Can we find opportunities for spiritual growth in the face of such obstacles?

Leaving the church, my thoughts drifted to an encounter I had with a young woman, Gail, who is trying to find her way in the world. When one is on a secure career and family track, it is easy to forget the frustration that accompanies not knowing what one is going to do with one's life. Then one may hear, voiced by a friend, the questions one too has asked in the search for meaning: Who am I most deeply? How can I express my unique gifts and talents? Where should I work? Will I meet someone to love and perhaps to marry me? What is my vocation? Is there really a grand design in which I have a special place? Gail described the misery of this transitional moment with various metaphors: "It's like walking through a muddy pool, climbing a rugged cliff, getting caught in a traffic jam. . . ."

She went on, "When, for instance, I have to travel bumper to bumper mile after mile, I feel irritable, impatient, mad at others and myself for taking the wrong road. Every inch I gain feels like a great accomplishment, yet I still have miles to go. The slightest opening compels me to switch from one lane to the other, but nothing really helps. I'm in a jam, and I can only go so far. I push ahead wherever possible, curse slow-moving cars, become aggressive. Stress mounts by the minute. I feel extremely defensive, unable to relax. Horns blow, rattling my nerves. Must I go on like this, agitated, restless, unsure? Where am I going? What am I doing? Is there no peace anywhere?"

Her life in its uncertainty is indeed like a traffic jam. She feels as if she has to haul herself over one hurdle after another. Any one of us can be caught in a transcendence crisis. We wonder where we have come from and where we are heading. Will there ever come a time when life is relatively worry-free, when we can, so to speak, cruise on a clear highway? Why is it that we no sooner disentangle ourselves from one traffic jam than we run into another?

Some of the hurdles we have to cross are external, like polluted air and the physical misery it provokes, but most of them are internal, like the upheavals that affect us physically, emotionally, communally. While there are many obstacles to spiritual growth upon which we could meditate, three in particular challenge us. They are *grandiosity,* or the temptation to vainglory; *guilt,* or the tendency to make ourselves and others feel miserable without the healing balm of mercy; and *gloom,* or the inclination to see darkness unredeemed by the light of God's goodness and glory. If we do not face these obstacles and, with the help of God's grace, gain freedom from them, they can drag us down into the disruptive pools of pride, perfectionism, and low-grade depression. The challenge before us is to see if these hindrances to ongoing formation in Christ can become helps in disguise.

To introduce the first obstacle, that of grandiosity, let me share the story of a contemplative religious who claimed to be experiencing extraordinary communications from God. When I had a speaking engagement in her community, the Prioress asked me if I would talk privately with this sister about her "visions." I expressed my hesitation to become involved on such a short-term basis but finally agreed to listen with discretion to what she had to say. That evening she appeared at my door—a petite woman with a pale complexion that contrasted sharply with rosebud lips and silky blue eyes, highlighted to my surprise with a tinge of bluish gray mascara, not exactly in keeping with the ascetic customs of the community. My suspicions about the authenticity of her experience increased in proportion to the haunting, fluttering attractiveness of her eyes. Her rendition of midnight visits from the Lord had the right blend of matter-of-factness and humility. Gentle modesty caused her to wonder why He had chosen her as the recipient of these revelations.

At a certain point my mind drifted from the details she articulated to the perfect actress she had become. I could see how someone without much background in the art of appraisal might be inclined to wonder if perhaps she had been chosen as one of God's messengers. Though her script could not have been improved upon, its validity beyond high drama was to my feeling an illusion. This sister, for whatever reason, needed to be the center of attention. Visions became the vehicle by which to attract the community's concern. Finally, she concluded her story. Lowering her delicately shadowed eyes, she awaited my response. I hardly knew what to say. Her self-image was as fragile as it was grandiose. Also, beneath her passive exterior, a volcano of unresolved passions seemed to be brewing. I wondered what it would take to cause that now dormant caldron to erupt uncontrollably.

In our short time together, I certainly could not begin to tap the complex layers of her case. I would recommend to the Prioress that the sister seek professional help, along with the support of a good spiritual director. The combination of therapy and direction might shed some light on the forest of fantasy in which she lived.

I thought it best not to discuss the visions directly but to ask about the quality of her daily life in the convent. What was her duty? She had been assigned to kitchen work. Did she like it? Not particularly. What did she like best? Liturgy, of course, and *lectio.* Yes, best of all she liked losing herself in the beauty of spiritual reading. I felt sad that she had not passed St. Teresa of Avila's test of mystical authenticity: Visions are fine, if they are from the Lord, but the test of their validity resides in leaving them behind—as St. John of the Cross says, in forgetting them all—and concentrating instead on how zealously one, so to speak, peels potatoes for supper.

I could not tell what Sister was thinking as she left the room. She thanked me for listening to her and seemed pleased by the good impression she had made upon me. I was impressed, but not as she assumed. She was then, and still remains, a powerful reminder that anyone involved in the delicate work of formative direction needs much study and experience. These inner realms are as explosive as dynamite. Hence, a director has to be in some ways as wise and cautious as a demolition expert.

When I confided to the Prioress the next day that we were playing with fire, I found much to my relief that she had already detected the smoldering flame. My confirmation enabled her to take action and arrange for Sister to receive the help we both knew she needed. I left the convent more convinced than ever that visions, like the olive trees outside the walls, had to be anchored in the firm soil of daily reality. The test of prayerful union had everything to do with peeling the potatoes.

The binds we get into are often traceable to our exalted ideals about how special we are, what astounding feats we can perform, the ways in which we can impress parents, colleagues, friends. To support the grandiose picture we have devised of ourselves, we may get into the habit of never saying no to anyone. We take on more and more tasks, as if we had the supreme power to accomplish them. When it turns out that we are not superhuman after all, only simple, ordinary people, our inflated self-image may be crushed. While we may experience the pain of ego-deflation, we may also witness the emergence of our unique personhood. The people we set out to please with grandiose schemes do not expect a spectacular performance. Mainly they are looking for someone who is humble, dedicated, and securely rooted in the Lord.

Grandiosity imprisons us in the pride form. Hiding under this "I can do it alone" fantasy is usually an insecure person who has never grown beyond the stage of being a people pleaser. What matters is looking good. And so, when concrete production breaks down, the blame is placed elsewhere because the apparent self must never fail. I struggle to keep up the facade of being in charge, knowing it all, never admitting a mistake.

The energy demanded to maintain this posture of individualized pride is immense. Sooner or later the facade begins to crumble. Grandiosity gives way under the routine pressures of ordinary living. In time, and with the proper help, I may learn to live in a relaxed way without having to do grand things to gain others' approval.

Anytime I deny my limits, I violate the law of humility. I no longer walk in the truth of who I am. I am a grandiose person if I consider it taboo to show signs of weakness. I must learn instead to rely on my own power, to prove to whoever is looking that I can control my environment completely. I need to be strong, to stay in charge, to use other people, if necessary, to serve my self-expanding plans. I seek power not only through material possessions like cars and clothes but also, and mainly, through dominating opinions, by insisting on having the last word. I avoid as much as possible the hidden life in favor of noticeable proofs of my self-worth. The hunger for acclaim is insatiable, making me adept at inventing attention-grabbing tricks.

Such grandiosity mercifully opens one in the end to crushing defeat. We can play God for only so long. Then our limits catch up with us. For instance, infidelity of a spouse teaches us that our marriage is not perfect, despite our pretense that it is. A runaway teenager reveals that our parenting has not always been honest, that our grandiose project of mother or father love blinded us to a troubled relationship. The boss's critique awakens us once and for all to the distinction between our promise to do everything and our actual productivity.

Freedom begins when we let go of these complex illusions of self-sufficiency and live a more truthful life, mindful at all times that God alone, not self, is our center. In His light, aware of His love for us as we are, we can do what we can in accordance with our limits and strengths, trusting that the fruits of our actions will speak for themselves.

Whenever we slip into grandiosity, we are reminded by the grace of defeat that without God we can do nothing. Our how-to-gain-approval tricks give way to a sense of wonder. God remains mindful of us despite our lack of remembrance of Him. Our attitude toward others becomes less controlling and more compassionate, like that of an old missionary, easily eighty, who received hundreds of people every other day. When a visitor asked him how he did it, he replied, "Each time I see God. I often see Him fifty times a day."

As I come to accept my limits and gifts, I am better able to separate the essential from the peripheral, to disentangle myself from yet another obstacle to spiritual deepening, that caused by excessive guilt feelings and a consequent inability to forgive myself as God forgives me. Some of the things for which I feel guilty are not really that significant. Why should I feel guilty about innocent slips from a self-imposed code of behavior? For instance, people do not always have to smile at me and say how great I am simply for doing my task well.

Guilt feelings that arise when I deviate from a perfectionistic mode of performance may be linked to fear of failure if I don't conform to certain prescribed expectations. Such feelings usually call forth a barricade of defenses. I feel compelled to make excuses when others admonish me. Because I cannot accept criticism or any sign of failure calmly, I tend either to withdraw into a protective cocoon or to force others to change their opinions to agree with mine. I feel secure only when they confirm me. I feel insecure if others express a view that is the opposite of my own.

I may also feel guilty as soon as I say no to someone, because my refusal does not fit into the ideal picture I have of myself as a cooperative, responsive, always available person. Guilt that emerges from perfectionistic tendencies is mainly false because I feel guilty about things that are impossible for me to be or to do at this time. When life becomes an attempt to compose a picture of the "ideal me," I may be driven to act in ways untrue to my deepest self. No wonder I disappoint the people I want to please most. The best way to gain freedom from the prison of this guilt-ridden image of individual perfection is to identify more fully with Christ, who loves me as the vulnerable person I am.

Each of us is unbalanced, neurotic, one-sided, and perfectionistic to a greater or lesser degree. Still, in God's eyes we are beautiful. In the midst of this self-torture, He calls us to be open and receptive to the purifying, illuminating, and unifying powers of the Spirit. We place our imperfect selves in the hands of Christ, whose saving mystery redeems us from the burden of sin and guilt. Through faith, our failings can become agents of transformation. God's grace can work through our defensiveness, insecurity, tension, and anxiety. He can turn these obstacles into honestly faced and transcended formation opportunities.

We can hinder our progress in the life of the spirit not only by grandiosity and guilt but also by gloom. Inordinate self-pity and chronic brooding can lead to low-grade depression. Steady loss of productivity, combined with chronic fatigue, results in an irritable, somber temperament. An eyebrow raised in criticism makes us cringe in self-blame or flare up in anger. Noticeable too may be a tendency to withdraw into our private, protective shell. We begin to separate ourselves from friends who want to help. We do not trust their good intentions. We may project onto them the hatred we feel for ourselves, becoming somewhat paranoid. We then harbor fantasies of persecution and convince ourselves that people are constantly talking about us behind our back, as if no one could understand what we are going through. We feel martyred by the pain we have to undergo and at the same time wonder if there is any justice in the world, since we do not deserve such prolonged persecution.

The only way to survive, we believe, is to keep our life under rigid control. If one peg crumbles, we fear the entire edifice of our carefully erected scheme will fall apart. In our gloomy state, help may be possible only if we are willing to seek good medical treatment, therapy, or spiritual direction.

We must try to listen to these symptoms and bring them to God for healing. He has already found us worthy of love despite our fallen condition. In the light of His redemption, we need not exaggerate our sorrow, worry, anxiety, or depression. If we can place our troubles against the wide horizon of divine mercy, their intensity will diffuse. This faith vision, enhanced by a sense of humor, by hearty laughter, will dispel the gloom and help us to shake off despondency. We are better able to wait patiently for the Lord to lift the shadow of sorrow. We trust Him enough to believe that He sends us suffering for a reason. Therefore, in desolation or consolation, our love remains the same. Such perseverance in hope helps us to move from concentration on gloom to loving longing for God. Feelings of desperation become reminders of the need to draw closer to the Lord.

Human beings learn more from symbols than from concepts. It is thus helpful to see sorrow as a pointer to the depression every human being suffers from time to time. Who among us does not have occasion to weep? God sends the message of mourning into our lives so that we can find one more graced opportunity to purge our hearts of egoism and allow Him to transform this sorrow into transcendent joy. We see in a mysterious way that our losses and failures have been blessings in disguise, benevolent messengers reminding us that only in the Lord can we find consolation that lasts.

This message was brought home to me as never before during a rainy, cloud-covered day in Tasmania, the southernmost state of Australia. Everything looked bleak, the air was chilly, and I felt that my melancholy mood perfectly matched the day. I was visiting Port Arthur, the ruins of a military compound and penal colony where over thirty thousand convicts were incarcerated from 1830 to 1877. Their crimes were as major as murder, as minor as stealing a loaf of bread to feed a starving family. Many were arrested in the British Isles, enchained like animals, and herded aboard ships, bound for what must have then seemed like the end of the earth. It was surely the end of life as they had known it. After months of sailing under inhuman conditions, the survivors disembarked on the desolate south coast of the Tasman Peninsula, only to be caged again in cells hardly big enough to contain a man.

The ruins seemed to echo with their cries. Was it the howling wind I heard or the ancient wail of the persecuted whose dust saturated this grass? As I walked in the cold mist from rampart to rampart, I wondered how these prisoners or any like them could have found meaning in life. I passed a spot called the "Isle of the Dead" with unmarked convict graves. As these men watched one another waste away, could they believe there was anyone who loved them? Could such stark and inhuman persecution be spoken of in the same breath as blessedness?

Suddenly I rounded a corner of the compound and stood still. There, rising in the middle of the fortress, was the framework of a Gothic chapel, its spires stretching upward in transcendent beauty. Though by now the mist had changed to rain, I felt as if the sun had broken through. I asked a guide to tell me about the history of the church. The design had been executed by one of the prisoners, who must have been a gifted architect. The drawings were done on scraps of paper with pieces of charcoal. A crew of fellow prisoners had erected the cathedral-like edifice. The bodies of these builders may have been enchained but not their spirits. Though they were starved, beaten, and buried, their dignity lived on in ancient arches.

Seeing that chapel changed my day. It became a symbol of the truth that in the midst of affliction the soul takes flight. One is free to find meaning no matter how severe the misery. In coping with obstacles, one finds opportunities for spiritual growth. When this meaning pivots on the mercy of

God, shores as ancient as those of the Tasman Sea proclaim a message of life that transcends the cruelest evidence of death. In the heart of darkness dawns a light whose shining never ceases.

CLOSING MEDITATION

Because He lives in us, the Lord is calling us to be one with Him in His basic disposition of grateful appreciation for the Father's goodness. He wants us to live in hope-filled abandonment to the benevolent presence of God behind every person, event, and thing in existence. Begin, therefore, to act always with appreciative abandonment to God so that this attitude may become second nature. Meditation in this sense must not be an occasional practice but a steady attempt to establish connections between everyday happenings and the holy. Decide to foster attentive presence to the divine reality, even when you feel spiritually arid. Make acts of gratitude that fill your soul with warm confidence in God's gracious goodwill in a vast and challenging array of circumstances. Then you may be able to pray with the same spirit that moved the Port Arthur prisoners to say in so many words:

> Lord,
> Death has no power
> To defeat your claim to life.
> Out of the soul's abandoned depths
> You hear cries agonized:
> Is there mercy enough
> To comfort our misery?
> Is there forgiveness enough
> To heal the breach

Caused by pride and perfectionism,
By defeat, depression, and despair?
What words are these
That console a heart
Grown faint with fear!
Come to me. Your burden
I shall carry. Your weakness
Shall become my strength.
Your light dappled with shadow
Shall shine forth like the sun.
My grace is enough for you.

Your words, O Lord, are hope
And consolation, sweet solace,
Oil poured out to soothe
Old wounds, to soften scars,
To turn these dark places
In my soul toward the stars.

8
Slowly We See

OPENING MEDITATION

How quickly time passes! If only we could stop the clock, move slowly, cease rushing. While we cannot block the passage of time, we can become more attentive to its meaning through meditation. Sit in a relaxed yet alert position with your eyes closed or focused on a familiar symbol and begin, perhaps in rhythm with your breathing, to repeat a text like "Jesus, mercy." One or two words are enough. Slowly· let them pass from your lips into your mind and down to your heart where you sense and respond to their meaning. As thoughts or images surface, simply repeat the text you've chosen, let them pass before your mind's eye in swift or slow motion, but don't fix your attention on them. Stay with the text while not resisting these distractions directly. Let them unravel as if you were watching them on film while really thinking of something else. Remain a disinterested observer of these emotions and movements until you are ready to return to normal activity. Regular use of this exercise will have an effect on the way in which you live. It will strengthen you to cope with the onslaughts of a swirling world.

My God! It's nearly eight o'clock. The concert starts in half an hour. I'm not even dressed. My heart beats faster. It's as if I'm on a rapid treadmill. Everything is spinning, turning. What a wild day this has been. I have to freshen my face, select the right clothes, rush out the door. Don't walk. Run. Gain time. I pray that I'll find a parking place as I pull into the lot of the Civic Center. The sign goes up: SORRY, FULL. I scream inwardly. Frantically I dash around the block to see if I can find an empty spot on the street. There's one. Inch in. Turn once, twice. Why can't I learn to parallel park? I'm going to make it. Lock the door. Remember the keys. I'm a wreck. Where are my friends? They're five minutes late. . . .

There is no stillness in such a scene. For some of us, to spin and turn continually, to operate on the edge of panic, becomes a way of life. Sooner or later this frenetic pace takes its toll. We pay the price of exhaustion, erosion of social presence, depletion of our prayer life. One look at our pocket calendar and we realize how overscheduled we are. Prayer means squeezing in a few words of praise or petition and moving on swiftly to the next appointment. Yet we long for something else, a quieter time, a slower pace. Pause for a moment, then, and remember the stillness . . .

. . . of a morning alone on the beach, minutes before sunrise, when earth, sea, and sky seem to be suspended in hushed expectation, silent except for the ebb and flow of the waves punctuated by a sandpiper's cry. . . .

. . . of a long walk along a country road flanked on either side by rolling hills covered with long, fawn-colored stalks of grass undulating in the breeze. . . .

. . . of a leisurely drive through the country from one sleepy town to the other, stopping by the general store for a cool drink and a friendly chat with the local folks.

These still times slow down the turning world and remind
us of life's finer moments—when we feel close to God, to
nature, to other people. It is possible to stop for a while, to
be with the Lord, to find time to pray. We believe what
ancient wisdom tells us in defiance of clock-bound, contemporary pressures:

There is a season for everything, a time for every occupation under heaven:

> A time for giving birth,
> a time for dying;
> a time for planting,
> a time for uprooting what has been planted.
> A time for killing,
> a time for healing;
> a time for knocking down,
> a time for building.
> A time for tears,
> a time for laughter;
> a time for mourning,
> a time for dancing.
> A time for throwing stones away,
> a time for gathering them up;
> a time for embracing,
> a time to refrain from embracing.
> A time for searching
> a time for losing;
> a time for keeping,
> a time for throwing away.
>
> (Eccl 3:1–6)

Events happen in time. Nothing escapes the reality of
past, present, and future, neither life nor death. In our culture, we are acutely conscious of clock time, of schedules,
appointments, durations. Other cultures, like the Asiatic

and the African, operate as if time is the servant of people and not the other way around. Time in a sense is space. It is the framework in which one lives from sunrise to sunset. One learns that if a meeting is to occur at ten in the morning, it may actually take place at noon. There is no use feeling uptight, because what happens, happens. A conversation with a person in a place like Tanzania, as my experience there taught me, always took precedence over an appointment. This attitude of letting be and enjoying life diminishes the tyranny of time and is certainly more conducive to a relaxed life of prayer.

However squeezed our schedules may be, the challenge is to transcend the pressure of time, not to make it an excuse to neglect prayer. Now is the appropriate time to go beyond the chronological realm. Think of the moments lovers share, wandering aimlessly along the shore, as a lazy afternoon melts into evening. Apply the same unpressured attitude to prayer. At such times, without thinking about it, we are on intimate terms with the Lord. His eternal presence pierces through the temporal sphere. Our finite lives are immersed in the infinite.

Practically speaking, three styles of prayer help us to integrate the timeless with time. I've designated these as the *prayer of passing time,* the *prayer of immediacy,* and the *prayer of presence.* Here is one example of each form:

———•◦•———

Lord, preserve me from the panic that ensues when I think of my days as rapidly passing. Where have the years gone? What do I have to show for them? Help me to see the aging process as a gentle passage from action to contemplation. Let your providential care for my life constitute my fondest remembrance. Show me as the years go by the surest path to follow so that one day we may be together in an eternal face to Face.

———•◦•———

Lord, here I am, running from store to store, shopping for the ingredients that go into tonight's meal. A list of orders a mile long hammers in my ear: Prepare the fish, clean the vegetables, make the dessert, set the table. . . . Help me to prepare a delicious meal so that I and my guests can celebrate the goodness of your creation.

How gracious it is, Lord, to be in your presence. Sharing with you this slowed-down pace fills me with peace. To see the stars, to feel the sand, to taste the salty breeze—this experience is too wonderful for words. Everything is in your hands, myself included. Whatever happens, let me live in the mystery of this contemplative awareness.

If we approach prayer as an integral part of daily life, there is really no time in which we cannot be praying. Perhaps this is what it means to pray always: simply to make room in our hearts for God wherever we may be. Then the world is no longer merely a place in which we work to the tune of a ticking clock. It is also the arena in which we worship. Prayer is thus not an occasional visit with God when we have the time, when we feel pained or under pressure. It is an all-encompassing orientation, a basic mood of being with Him in love, knowing that even if we distance ourselves from Him, He remains near to us.

Prayer is a gift, which calls forth in us attitudes of expectancy and receptivity. As we open ourselves to God, we allow Him to touch and move us on every level of our being. True prayer is not produced by controlled meditative techniques or intellectual reasoning alone. It is a gift of grace, not attainable as such by human efforts. Prayer begins when we offer our entire being to the One whose forming mystery we seek to embody in our day-to-day situation.

I remember in this regard the sister who prepared me for

my first communion. She was a gentle, loving nun who in-
stilled in us first graders the sense that we were personally
cared for by the Lord. His presence shone through her
whole being, both in and out of the classroom. In those
days, religion was taught through the Baltimore Catechism
and, thanks to this sister, I've never forgotten its opening
reminder that we were made to know, love, and serve God
in this world that we may be happy with Him forever in
eternity. This text impressed me deeply. Its lived meaning
was embodied in my first Christian teacher. God was her
joy, and I wanted Him to become mine, too.

I still have the petite white prayer book that was part of
our communion kit. Into it my mother tucked a photo of
me in my little gown with no front teeth and a grin from ear
to ear. I was truly happy, and, without stretching memory
too far, I think I experienced the presence of God warming
my heart. The special nearness I felt in church that day
brought Him more personally into my life from then on.
Sister counseled us to converse with Christ about everything. He was interested in our friends, our progress in
school, our relationship with our family, our times of work
and play. Her words went together with my mother's cus-
tom of calling upon various saints to cover trials and tri-
umphs: Lucy for eye trouble, Blaise for the throat, Jude for
impossible causes, Christopher for safety on the road, An-
thony for things lost that had to be found. Her favorite,
faith-filled phrases were: "What's to be will be," "God
knows what He's doing," "His will be done," "Be patient
and everything will turn out fine."

A major obstacle to this practice of presence is sheer human pride. To pray means precisely to bypass my egocentric
self and open my heart humbly to God. Pride inclines me to
cling to my plans and projects and to use prayer as an occasion to obtain God's stamp of approval. Though I pray, as
in the Our Father, "Thy kingdom come, Thy will be done,"

too often what I secretly mean is, "My will be done." I live in the expectation of success as I see it, not in surrender to God's providential plan for my life. The focus of prayer is more on self in isolation than on self in relation to Him in whom I live and move and have my being.

We may go so far as to equate the efficacy of prayer with the amount of worldly achievements or possessions we have amassed. We imagine that our merit in heaven is in direct proportion to our accomplishment on earth. We cling to the letter of the law and boast of our obedience while ignoring its spirit. We make sacrifices to look good but neglect the evolvement of a loving attitude. This mentality may lead us to amass projects of transformation or prayer techniques that fail in the end because they are generated by a self that refuses to accept its own vulnerability. We surround ourselves by achievements or possessions, relying on these for security and proof of holiness. We look to things outside of God to make us feel spiritually secure instead of to God himself as our only ultimate fulfillment.

Another obstacle is that we studiously avoid the cross and equate spirituality with good feelings. We instinctively resist anything that is unpleasant. We find it hard to believe that occasions for grace may be found in a failed business negotiation, a family disagreement, a long wait in the doctor's office. The holiness we want makes us feel good; it does not challenge us to make the best of difficult deals, to welcome irritation and displeasure as potential sources of redemption from power, pleasure, and possession. What seems contrary to our expectations of satisfaction is labeled a hindrance to be overcome by human effort alone. How well I remember making this mistake as a child.

Like many Italian men, my father thought that regular churchgoing was mainly for women. For the longest time I didn't say anything about going to Mass on Sunday without him. Then, not long after my grandmother's death, when I became more sensitive to the meaning of a faith commitment and my desire to live it as she did, I decided that my first important mission would be to set my father straight by getting him to go to Mass regularly.

My tactics were hardly subtle. I began my campaign by lecturing him on the value of attending Mass on ordinary Sundays, not merely on important holy days. This approach only served to increase his stubbornness and to remind him to remind me of my insolence in regard to judging others. He had his own way with God, and I was entitled to mine. Knowing I had reached a dead end with the lecture route, I tried to shame him into attendance, appearing on Sunday morning in church garb, missal in hand, refusing even water to keep the fast, and saying, when he would offer to drive me, that I preferred to walk. Self-righteous faith never produces good fruit, as I soon found out. He refused to broach the subject and, as a newly charged missionary, I felt a total failure.

Then one Sunday I arose earlier than usual. Mother was already in the kitchen. I saw Daddy lying in bed reading the paper. I stood at the doorway in customary vigilance. He looked up with a glance that told me he did not want another lecture. Tears welled up in my eyes. I said I only wanted to be in church with him and that if he didn't go, I wouldn't go either. We looked at each other for a long moment, two stubborn Italians. Then he opened his arms, embraced me wordlessly, and told me to go and get dressed. I saw him turn back to the paper and concluded that God would have to take over his case because I had failed miserably.

A while later I came out of my room and went into the kitchen for breakfast. Mother was smiling but not saying a word. I could hear Daddy in the bathroom singing and shaving. He came out, nicely dressed, finished his toast and coffee, glanced at his watch, and casually said, "Isn't it time for church?" From that Sunday onward, he seldom missed Mass. I sensed then spiritual truths that the Lord has confirmed over and over again: When we get out of the way with our great ego plans, He has room to work; when we witness to faith, instead of preaching about it, people will respond in ways beyond expectation; when we offer another person love, love is enkindled in turn; when we cease judging others, they cease judging us.

In our blindness to spiritual meaning, we seek functional solutions to the suffering we feel. We don't pause to consider the deeper symbolism of what is happening, namely, our dependence on a power greater than us. We hate to face our vulnerability. We resent having to wait for something to be resolved in ways over which we have little or no control. Whether we seek the easy way out or escape in busy work, we resist the ordinary trials of daily life as openings to prayer. We miss the chances they grant us to purify pride and the ignorance of transcendent formation it breeds.

A different feeling comes over us when we empty ourselves before God in prayer so that He can fill us with new energy. We sit down quietly. Though the events of the day flow through our mind, we turn our attention to Him. We share the same space, the same time, in wordless, loving awareness. As cares and concerns drift away, He fills our hearts with newfound faith and assurance. His loving touch penetrates our being as fragrant perfume saturates a sponge. It is as if the stream of His love swells and swells until it sweeps into the farthest corners of our life. We feel less resistant to His invasion, freed from inordinate attachments to the little gods of our making, ready to be His instruments for good in the world. Reflecting on our joys, disappointments, trials, and frustrations in this mood, we perceive them as unexpected graces calling us to discover new facets of God's mysterious, unspeakable love. In the stillness of this moment, we remember His presence. We listen to the voice of our Beloved, inviting us to be with Him a while, waiting patiently, growing in faith, overflowing with gratitude.

When we view a grand mountain reflected majestically in a still lake, a sunset dropping steadily behind a calm blue bay, we are led spontaneously to a prayer of praise. Creation sings of the splendid exuberance of its Creator. What a wondrous interplay of sun, sea, and sky. Nature awakens us, as no other experience can, to the sheer artistry of God. Prayer becomes like play: carefree, creative, noncompetitive. It is like listening to music, strolling in a park, lying in the sun. In this unrushed moment, we can renew and deepen our relationship with the Lord. We see our life not as a collection of petty needs but as part of the immense drama of creation in which we have a small but vital role to play. Though we may periodically lose our sense of direction and take a more roundabout way to God, we know that in some way we already possess that for which we are longing. Even if we make the wrong choice and lose the path for a while, God does not reject us. He is able to encompass our mistakes and, in a mysterious way, to incorporate them into the economy of salvation.

Such moments of contemplative dwelling take us out of the whirlwind of worldly consumption and production. They create a still space in which we can be ourselves before God with no hidden agendas. We feel quiet within and without. For however brief a duration, anger subsides, emotion cools. We are lifted beyond impulse and ambition to transcendent aspiration. Restored by this view of the order and beauty of creation, we can return refreshed and renewed to the inevitable disorder and ambiguity of daily labor.

This pause for prayer and reflective meditation unquestionably enhances the quality of our workaday participation. Far from detracting from our functionality, spirituality heightens the effectiveness and attractiveness of our action

in the world. Because there is less and less separation between silence and service, worship and work, we can find
time throughout the day to slow down the turning world
while we turn toward the eternal.

CLOSING MEDITATION

Pretend that you are viewing the world through the lens of a
slow-motion camera. Move as slowly and steadily as possible
around a small space, not missing one detail. By analogy,
think of how the Lord tends each minute and cosmic marvel
of creation. Take a plant leaf, turn it to the light, and behold
its veined beauty, its perfect form. Study it in awe until you
feel drawn deeply into the mystery of formation in and
around you. Let the wonder of God's world astound you. Let
it quell the stress and tension in you so that with heartfelt
longing you can pray:

> Quiet me, Lord,
> Like a child curled up
> On its mother's lap,
> Like a deer poised
> In silent expectation,
> Ready to leap at twig's snap
> To sheltered safety.
> Slow me down
> So I can see
> Sunrise over spring-green trees,
> Ocean's wave splashed upon volcanic rock,
> Leaves golden with autumn splendor,
> A young man's face, an old man's fingers.
> Still the rush
> So I can smell and taste and touch

Freshly baked, buttered bread,
Logs bright, burning red,
Birds feeding, kites flying,
All soaring manifestations
Of your mysterious creation.
Let these gifts like cosmic fire
Purify anxious panic.
Lead me, Lord, ever longing
To voiced and voiceless,
Present, praising,
Never ceasing
Prayer.

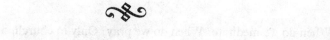

9
Lessons from Life

When do we meditate? When do we pray? Only in church, or when tragedy strikes, or as a matter of routine morning and night? Sadly, we miss the signals of transcendence sent out continually from the emission station of everyday life. Resolve not to let these opportunities pass you by. Become more alert to God's call in the course of each day's unfolding. Become a person who frequently questions, thanks, converses with and worships God. Let His presence become the horizon of your actions. Build a hermitage in your heart. In quiet times, retreat there so that you may emerge refreshed, restored, ready to accept whatever responsibility He gives you. Give your relationship with Him the priority it deserves. Then you will meet God not merely on special occasions but in the immediacy of each situation.

When my mother celebrated her seventy-fifth birthday, I asked her if she would share with me the main values by which she lived. There were two of them: working and loving. Hard work, she affirmed, is good for the body, and love is essential for the soul. These are the disciplines that make one a true disciple. Work enables her to be of service to anyone who asks for help, to exercise her creativity whether she is planting a summer garden, preparing a meal, or completing an oil painting. She loves others and God with her whole being, giving generously of her time, energy, and talents. She listens to the lessons life teaches and says she is never too old to learn.

These two disciplines are Mother's shortcuts to a long, healthy, and holy life. One thinks of other practices that enable us to be more disciplined in our approach to God, such as silence, formative reading, meditation, and prayer. These disciplines, like other good habits and virtuous acts, are shortcuts to discipleship. They enable us to become more like the Lord whom we follow. By analogy, we know that the more habitual certain practices become, like dressing, cooking, or cleaning, the more we free our minds for reflection or conversation. We gain time to pursue excellence in the field of our choice. An old gardener once taught me an unforgettable lesson in regard to this question of discipline for the sake of growing in more loving dedication to the Lord.

Sebastian lived across the street from my cousin. He kept a beautiful garden and took pride in his vegetables. When summer came, he supplied the neighbors with peas and corn, tomatoes and string beans. After his wife, Martha, died, the garden became his main consolation. Despite a serious heart condition, he hoed and tended the plants throughout the growing season. They became his dearest companions. He talked to them, and in their own way they responded to him.

I recall thinking when I met him that his face looked like a garden. The skin was burned as brown as midsummer soil. There were little furrows running from the corners of his eyes to the tip of his chin. He had a face full of character and strength that beamed with care for the good organic

vegetables he grew. I walked beside him during those days I
visited my cousin, watching while he raked and pruned each
tender plant. We did not talk much. When we did, the main
topic was the weather and, after that, garden pests. Once in
a while he would point to the pacemaker in his chest, which
he called "God's shortcut to Sebastian's health." With the
wonder of a child, he would describe the miracle sewn inside his skin that kept him alive.

It is only now, as I reminisce, that I realize how meeting
Sebastian was a milestone in my life. What made him so
significant? Surely nothing he said, for we spoke of the most
common things. Perhaps what stays with me is his gentle,
dedicated presence. He was disciplined, strong, old in years
yet a child at heart, simple yet profound like a desert father.
He learned lessons from the earth. His wisdom came from
life, and life is the best teacher.

When he showed me his "shortcut," he said, "You see,
Susan, if this heart of mine stops, nothing else I love can
grow. A lot of my friends have died. They were afraid of
city doctors, but I wasn't. I let them operate, and now I've
got a miracle inside me. That's why this garden keeps on
growing."

I gathered as we walked together that the deepest reason
Sebastian took care of himself was because he believed the
Lord cared for him and wanted him to tend that garden. It
was easy to see that he and God were the best of friends.
They discussed what kind of fertilizer to use, when to rotate
the crops, what neighbors were most in need of the produce.

I remember also how Sebastian handled his tools. He
never grasped them harshly. He guided them so that they
could do their work. It was as if he trusted his tools to do
exactly what they had been made to do once he set them in
motion, not unlike the way a writer trusts the pen, or an
artist the paintbrush and pallet. Trust in his tools symbol-

ized the trust he had in life and in the Hand that guided its every turn.

From Sebastian I learned the real value of disciplines as shortcuts to discipleship. When we know where we are going and the fastest way to get there, we can afford to be less rushed, less grasping, less aggressively in control. This lesson bears on every activity we do, from sweeping rugs to writing, from tending house plants to teaching. Whenever I forget the things Sebastian taught me and fall into an arrogant pattern, I pause to remember the way my friend held his rake and hoe. I relax and try to let his care be expressed in the way my hands work.

I recall the first few times I baked bread. Without a recipe to follow, but with the encouraging presence of my mother, who knew every shortcut in the book, I actually produced five crusty golden loaves instead of the expected hard lumps of baked flour. I could never have gotten that far without the benefit of a time-tested discipline. Similarly, we have to establish certain routines that ready us, with the grace of God, to live a richer spiritual life. Stillness, listening, meditative reading, and keeping a journal are a few examples. Practicing these exercises helps us to grow in nearness to God. They shorten our path to the transcendent.

A seamstress who has mastered her art does not feel anxious or tense when she has to do something difficult like pleat a skirt. She knows what and what not to do to avoid wasting material or doubling her labor. When the skirt is complete, she can stand back and admire her work, delighted that she has made something beautiful, happy to pass on her skills to others. Her disciplined presence to dressmaking is enriched each time she listens to the deeper meaning of what she does. Within routine functions and circumstances, she hearkens to the call of love that binds her to God. This heightened sensitivity to the spiritual underpinnings of all persons, events, and things is a mark of true discipleship. It is surely a shortcut to the Lord.

A disciplined life manifests a distinct deliberateness. It moves with diligent care toward the prize it seeks: union with God. We want to go to Him by the shortest route possible, though fallen human nature usually leads us astray. Like St. Paul, we want to forget the past and strain ahead for what is still to come. Like him, we, too, must go forward on the road that has brought us to where we are.

In this regard, I will never forget the story told to me by a businessman I met during a retreat. It illustrates the turn to God that gives one a new sense of resoluteness so that life once again has purpose, meaning, and direction. Prior to the event that marked the turning point, Peter would be upset by the most trifling things. A mildly trying day at work would make him so tense he needed a couple of martinis. To make up for neglect, he would work overtime, swallow pep pills, and spend fewer evenings with his family. He either did practically nothing or tried to accomplish everything at once. He could never relax. He couldn't trust others. He felt increasingly depressed and one day ended up in the hospital in a state of nervous exhaustion. This was paradoxically the event of ego-desperation he needed to come to his senses.

Lying in a hospital bed, he had the first chance in years to reflect on his life's journey thus far. He realized that his classic mistake was always having to be in charge, even of his relationship with God. Peter had never really surrendered to love. Was it not high time to let go and entrust himself totally to God's care? He stopped trying to carry the world on his shoulders. Against this larger horizon, he saw the way he had to follow. It was not a question of going from one extreme to the other, from overwork to irresponsibility, but of acting in a calmer, more collected way with good common sense. He told himself, for example, that if a contract does not get signed today, it will probably be negotiated tomorrow. He had to delegate responsibility to others so that he could go home on time. He would set aside a few moments each day to be alone with God.

This change of heart had repercussions on every level of Peter's life. Physically, he was much healthier because he was less tense. Mentally, he was able to think more clearly because he had a keener sense of what was right and wrong in the situation. Emotionally, he was an easier person to live with, not swinging so fast from high to low moods but maintaining more balance. Spiritually, he experienced being accepted by God as he was, with all his faults and failings. He no longer looked so anxiously and scrupulously at himself because he knew God was faithful to him and was unremitting in His expression of mercy.

There are many such graced occasions in our spiritual life, and it is always wise, as Peter found out, to follow them. Self-knowledge or humility is a deep grace, provided that I can see through my egoism and turn to the Lord. His wisdom is often invisible to the eyes of the world. By contrast, with eyes of faith, we see Him as the inmost reality and origin of every created form of life. When we are illumined from within by the divine light, we no longer watch ourselves as lonely soldiers on a vast battlefield of life where people count for little. Rather, we know we are held by the Holy, cherished in a special way as His chosen.

Detachment is another shortcut to spiritual deepening insofar as it frees us *from* possessive attitudes and egocentric desires. It consequently frees us *for* greater attachment to God as the ultimate source of all that is good. Multiple desires and subtle idolatries give way to one longing to live in union with God and in trusting surrender to His merciful care. We resign past, present, and future to His guidance in the conviction that His love will last forever. Oneness with Him prevails in twilight, deep darkness, and dawn. We know that He is the beginning and end of our journey. The sufferings we undergo on the long road to eternity pale in comparison to the peace and joy He promises.

The great witness in my life to this style of discipleship is and remains my maternal grandmother, Elizabeth. While she was living, and in the end as she awaited death—slow in coming because of a painful, prolonged cancer—she was the epitome of a faithful woman. Many are the occasions when I remember her loving, laughing presence. I had known for some time that she was dying, but the finality of this fact had not fully registered. Only twelve years old at the time, I clung to the belief that she would recover, that I would feel her arms around me once more, that I would inhale the life-giving, freshly baked bread scent of her body and bask in the lightheartedness of her unquenchable humor. I wanted to feel blessed again by the winks full of meaning she reserved for me alone. I knew that of all the grandchildren she favored me the most, for with me she could share without words the depth of her faith. Now her light was growing dim. Nothing, not even the full force of my love, could hold back the dark.

The night she died—this uneducated, illiterate peasant woman who mothered eleven children, who was a paragon of faith, whose Christian witness I shall never forget—that night I could not weep. The tears came two days later, wet as rain falling on the earth in which she was buried. On the evening of her passing, perhaps to distract my attention, my aunt, a beautician, took out her scissors and said she would cut my hair. I offered no resistance. I had long, dark brown tresses that had only been trimmed, never shorn. I allowed her to clip away until the hair curled around my ears. When my mother saw what my aunt had done, she went into hysterics, but the hair lay in piles on the rug. Maybe those shorn tresses symbolized more than I realized at the time of my beloved grandmother's departure. Just as there was no way of putting them back on my head, so there was no way of bringing her back from the dead.

My parents plunged us back into life. They gave my brothers and me a good home. My father was a hardworking contractor, my mother his right hand. She was always there when my brothers and I came home from school, preparing a tasty snack and sharing our problems. She preached by living her beliefs, by demanding honesty, generosity, and a sense of responsibility. My father needed some coaxing at times to be in church, but, externals aside, he too had a strong faith and seemed attuned to God's will in his life. He maintained a devotion he had received from his mother, the praying of the rosary. All in all, I would have to say that I grew up in an atmosphere of Christian discipline, but that fact does not explain my intense—at times painfully intense—awareness of God, nor does it explain my early and unshakable conviction that He had a plan for my life that I would be free to accept or refuse.

Because I witnessed firsthand the faith of my grandmother, who accepted God's plan for her life in the face of insurmountable odds, I, too, would say yes to the divine design of my life. Because she did not refuse God's love, even when it took the form of pain, neither would I. Of course, these resolutions were only in seed form at the time of her death. Only later, in looking back upon the events of that period, would I discover how much her witness of Christian discipleship meant to me.

A few months later, I had my first fight with God. Somewhere, perhaps at a school retreat or during one of the many hours I spent alone in my room reading, I began voicing this promise to live my life in tune with His grand design—the plan on which Grandmother seemed to base her faith. What I didn't realize was what that assent might mean. Though I tried my best to be like all the other children at school, I knew inside that I was different. I giggled

when the girls did, even if I did not find their jokes that
funny. I experienced my first crush on a boy who seemed a
bit more sensitive than the rest. I studied hard and received
good to excellent grades. On the surface, all was well, but
inside I knew I was being called, led, urged, prompted to be
aware of God. This awareness made me feel strange. I wondered if the other girls thought as much about God as I did.
It was not a question of going to religion classes, though I
liked these well enough. What puzzled me was the feeling
that though I sensed God inside me, I did not feel attracted
to the convent as a few of the girls in my class did.

One day I had it out with God. I released my anger and
confusion about life and death. I wanted Him to answer the
great questions or to leave me alone. I felt old before my
time. I wanted out of the implicit pact I had made with Him
at my grandmother's death, the promise to be faithful—
whatever that might mean. All it meant was suffering from
a feeling of inner solitude, pretending to conform to peer
notions of fun when I really felt alone and confused, overly
conscious of right and wrong, wondering what to do when
the face of Christ appeared to my mind's eye and His sad,
gentle eyes beckoned me to I knew not where.

I remember walking up to the end of our yard and beg-
ging God, then shouting at Him, to let me alone, to let me
be "normal," free to go my way, to be like everyone else, to
cease marching to a different drummer. When the last
words poured forth, I felt drained of emotion but simultaneously at peace, as if God had confirmed my faith by allowing me to be exactly who and where I was. I felt Him
stepping back so I could grow, while assuring me that, for
better or worse, I was His own. The meaning of these two
events, Grandmother's death and the backyard bout, has
never left me. They form an intricate part of my Christian
childhood. Bits and pieces of this early formation thus

gather around these seminal events of life, death, and re-birth.

One of my more pleasant memories of discipleship has to do with reception of the sacrament of confirmation—that symbolic ritual that marks the shift from adolescence to the onset of Christian adulthood. It was our responsibility to choose a confirmation name and to explain the reason for our choice to the class. The name I chose was Veronica, which was the name of the woman who wiped the face of Jesus as He walked the way of the cross to Golgotha. Little is known about her—only this one act of womanly compassion. What she did seemed so spontaneous, so kind. For some reason I could identify with her bold act to console the Lord. I would have liked to do the same thing, to show Him how much I cared, to help Him feel at that lonely moment less isolated, less despised. I wanted Him to know He had a friend. Veronica's reaching out to touch Him, as well as His allowing this intimate contact, spoke to me of the friendship I craved from the Lord. To receive the sacrament of confirmation and this new name sealed the bond of our togetherness in a new way and made me feel that He and I were one in our desire to obey the Father's will. I would be Veronica wiping His tears and, at my most vulnerable moments, He would wipe mine.

My spiritual life grew in the light of this unfolding dialogue I had with the Lord. I took seriously the friendship between us that had been confirmed in the sacrament and continued asking Him the disciple's basic question, "What would you have me do?"

I experienced a lot of aloneness over the next few years, sensing keenly at times that "different factor" that I could never dismiss. There was the surface me and the private me: the girl with leadership and verbal gifts and the young woman who felt touched by the Lord and determined to serve Him, whatever that might mean. Little did I know then that the seeds of faith and fidelity, planted in childhood, would lead me to a ministry in the field of spirituality and to a calling to the single life in the world. God has many surprises in store for those who love Him and are willing to take the risk of surrendering to His will. He leads us through many deaths, many decisions, many rebirths. The journey begun in childhood continues to the end of time.

CLOSING MEDITATION

As we follow God in diverse and unexpected situations, we learn a lesson only life can teach. His will is not, except in rare cases, a clear-cut command but a gentle, challenging invitation to live the Gospel wherever we are, whatever we do. Whether at home or office, at recreation or work, we are to hear His voice, heed His appeal, accept His challenge. In this sense, every time is a good time for meditation. We do not have to wait until the mood is upon us or until we have a special favor to ask. Try, therefore, to incorporate these directives into your daily routine. In fact, pray always, that is to say, always live in openness to the mystery of God's forming presence. Be receptive to its ineffable yet effective reminders that you are never alone. God is with you if you remain in His grace. Because of this gifted relation, you and I dare to say:

> O Trinity divine,
> Father, Son, and Holy Spirit,
> Your love sustains me
> At each turn of the road.
> Gently and lovingly,
> You awaken my soul.

You await my turning
And forgive my weakness,
You never forget
The likeness between us.

The most common acts
Of breathing and eating,
Speaking and praying,
Caring and teaching,
Become invitations to inner awakening,
For seeing, though darkly,
Your outpouring of graces.

Surrender to your holy will
Frees me from worry,
Lets me grow still.
In these many faces
I see that most dear,
In these many voices,
Only yours do I hear.

Make me mindful of what Christ would do,
How He would respond on each occasion.
What care and compassion would He manifest?
How can He best become the source of my yes?
Yes to the Father,
Yes to the Son,
Yes to the Spirit,
To all three in one.

This yes is the imprint you've made on my soul,
The flame of love that burns deeply within,
The yes that makes possible the no to sin.
No to the old me
Gives way to the new,
Empty of self, ready for you.

10
Meditation in Motion

ॐ

Friends drift away. Children grow up. Governments rise and fall. Life changes. Life continues. We cannot stop the flow, but we can find the deeper meaning of it through meditation. By now you know that this gift must not be confined to a set time but accomplished while you are in motion. You come in this way to live in meditative reflection. Notice these results. There is more harmony between your faith and your formation. What you believe is an expression of who you are. What you give to others is mirrored in the way you live. Think of a flowing river. In other than flood conditions, its swift movement is guided by solid embankments. It rushes on in accordance with a distinct direction. If you were to place your life in that river, you too would be pushed on by its force, over obstacles, toward the sea. You would be carried along a certain route until one day you would drop into the ocean of God's love. Here our analogy ceases. For unlike the river, which is entirely absorbed in the magnitude of seawater, you and I remain unique persons, utterly different from and dependent upon God yet in a mysterious way united to Him. Meditate on this mystery of oneness and uniqueness. It is a gift appreciated more and more as we practice meditation in motion.

❧

Movement, regularity, direction—these traits are as characteristic of meditation as they are of life in general. For what is meditation but a direct, regular movement of mind and heart toward the Holy? In meditation, we move from point to point, reflecting, dwelling, coming to a standstill, then moving on, as we do in the patterns that compose ordinary living. For what is life itself but a long journey from the unknown to the familiar to a greater unknown?

Once we are beyond the security of childhood, our minds begin to expand with new ideas and dreams. Our emotions enlarge as for the first time we know loneliness, sweet longing, sorrow, and wonder. We move from adolescence to adulthood, assuming more responsibility; thinking through our formation journey step by step; making decisions that are congenial with who we are and compatible with our situation. We strive to be compassionate and to exercise our competence in a chosen profession, to enjoy recreation, to catch ourselves before we overwork and ruin our health. We want to cultivate the good soil of self-respect and charity while uprooting the weeds of violence and narcissism. We long to discover and develop the hidden treasures of silence, solitude, relaxed spiritual reading, contemplative prayer, and wholehearted service.

Gradually, as our journey through life moves to closure, we want to peel away the excess baggage and travel more lightly; to empty out of our lives, as we clean house in the spring, the accumulated dross of divisive prejudices, angry impulses, greedy ambitions, unrealistic expectations—all the traces of pride and power that separate us from consonance with Christ.

Once there was a missionary who worked in the mountainous villages of a remote region in Mexico. The people he served were able to attend Mass only once every three months. Word got out that the priest was finally coming to the farthest point in his territory. Unbeknown to him, the people there were suffering from the worst blight of bugs attacking their meager crops that they had experienced in years.

When they knew that Mass would be celebrated, they prepared themselves for the journey, which for some entailed a walk of three days. Before leaving, whole families went into the fields and collected as many bugs as they could and put them in a variety of jars and cans. An altar had been erected in front of the village church, since the tiny structure itself could not hold the hundreds of people in attendance. The priest watched as the people assembled from dawn to dusk, bringing not only themselves and their families but also container upon container of bugs.

Before Mass began, he asked one of the village leaders to explain what was happening. The latter said with childlike faith, "Padre, when these bugs are in the presence of the Holy God, they will see how bad it is to eat our crops and they will return to the desert." Priest and people and insects celebrated the Eucharist as night fell. The next morning all but the local villagers had disappeared. The jars of blessed bugs had been buried in a huge grave. Weeks later the missionary learned that the corn crop was the best in years. The pests had disappeared without a trace.

After a long day, I have noticed when I drive home from work how soothing is the sound of the regular turning of the wheels. They rotate like the passing of days, moving on with a steady pace. The sound is stilling like a regular heartbeat, and I find myself growing calmer as I listen to it. I am struck anew by the importance of routine in our lives. We need these daily rituals to cushion us against the bombardment of new challenges, unfamiliar tasks, fresh insights into ourselves and our relationships with which we cannot quite cope. I must admit that there are many times when I simply need to get away from it all, to escape to a quiet place and listen to my surroundings, to soothing sounds.

There is a hidden power that appeals to the spirit in the regularity and order of ritual. This explains our attraction to liturgical participation, to symphonic music, to magnificent art. We need to be elevated beyond functional pursuits and competitive exertion to the plane of aesthetic beauty. The ordered cadence of chant, the rhythmic flow of the liturgy, the periodic pealing of church bells—these sounds lift our spirits. They remind us of the regular intake and outflow of breath, the aspiration and inspiration of prayer. Some experiences stay with us as a radiant example of aesthetic transcendence. Nazareth is one of them for me.

For years, through scripture reading, the world of this tiny village had lived in my memory as if I had at one time been there. The hidden life of the Lord seems to the human mind so foolish. Why, the one time He was on earth, did He choose to remain in obscurity in an unknown place? What is the meaning of Nazareth for us today? Was the Lord communicating the importance of the hidden life, the richness of the ordinary? Now the dream of being there was coming true. At last I had arrived in the town where Jesus lived. I had been traveling in the Holy Land, saving the best for last, the beauty of the Upper Galilee.

The climb to the village is steep, the view magnificent. If one loved nature, its green, red, beige, gold glory, then this would be the place to be born, for Nazareth is part of a valley of wondrous contrasts. Mountainous ravines, high ridges, tall cypress trees, low blooming bushes—it is a feast for the eye, a land surely touched by the finger of God. The main streets and squares of Nazareth are given over to the merchants and the tourists, but one can find any number of quiet places for meditation.

My first stop was at the Basilica of the Annunciation, a focal point toward which the pilgrim spontaneously gravitates. I was in time that Sunday morning for the ten o'clock service. The church is overwhelming in size and color. The Virgin is celebrated in artwork and mosaics donated by many different nations. The liturgy in Latin was regal, impressive, truly moving to tourists and townspeople.

After Mass I found myself longing to be in a setting where I could feel closer to Jesus of Nazareth. This ritual reminded me of what was to become His public mission. I wanted to experience something of the life that was more private. So I left the basilica and began wandering through the streets, toward the homes of ordinary people. Here was the Nazareth I had imagined: narrow lanes, tiny stone houses, doorways one had to stoop down to enter. I walked not knowing what I might find. The children with their olive skin, dark eyes, and straight black hair gave me a glimpse of what Jesus might have looked like as a boy.

Around the corner appeared a little girl, a lovely child of seven or eight in a white bridal dress, feted by her parents and the whole family. Seeing her brought me back to my own first communion day. Several other young children appeared behind her to complete the procession. They emerged with their parents and relatives from the small archway and courtyard of a Greek church. The scene was so homey, so inviting, I had to go in. The communion service was over, but the parish priest was at the font baptizing a baby by immersion in the holy water. The faces of the assembled family were full of joy. One child had stayed in the church to have some photos taken. She wanted to pose for me and then with me. In the meantime the baptismal procession paraded around the tiny church with candles aglow. It was a lively, reverent, joyous scene. The ritual was far less dignified than the one I had attended in the basilica, but it had its own beauty and charm, its own heartwarming inspiration. Maybe the Lord and His family had participated in such events in accordance with their faith tradition.

Here, in this neighborhood of Nazareth, my longing to experience something of Jesus' hidden life was fulfilled as never before. I understood by looking at the children why He had chosen to remain an ordinary person for so many years. He became one of us. He lived in and sanctified the everydayness of things. He taught us by His living example that life is rarely a high ritual, that if we are to find its meaning, it must be in the lowly order and beauty of daily routine.

The direction we seek is revealed not in dramatic ways but in quiet drives from one place to the next, as we move with faith and trust from familiar to unknown paths. We want our lives to mean something, and thus we ask frequently, Where have I been, where am I now, where am I going? These questions are not uttered in idle curiosity but with heartfelt concern. We do not want our lives to be wasted. We want to believe that we have made a difference in the world. God will not desert us in this quest for direction if we ask Him to be our friend and guide. He has placed us on this earth for a reason, and He wants us to find it. No life, however sickly and unproductive it may be, is wasted in His eyes.

Our deepest truth, our highest nobility, resides in the fact that we are created after His image, in His own likeness. Nothing can diminish this bond of unity sealed by His love for us from the beginning. We are free to resist this love or to flow with it. One way leads to the image of self as a lonely fighter in an endless battle that no one wins. The other way leads to the self-image of a noble, beloved human being whose mission in life is twofold: to surrender to the mystery in loving obedience, and to use one's gifts to the full to serve others as God's instrument.

Surrender and service, quiet repose and active cooperation—these are the dual forces that drive us forward, ever transcending. When the road is rough, as in times of illness or death, we have no choice but to lift ourselves and others into the light of the Holy. Only in appreciative abandonment to the mystery of formation can we find meaning in such tragic revelations of human finitude. We must not wait for events that constitute situations of limit to practice surrender. Rather, we are to learn the art of lifting everyday happenings into this light, events such as a glorious moment when tension is released and we celebrate recreation; a gourmet meal as well as a picnic lunch; a glass of lemonade on a hot August afternoon; a sip of wine with someone we love; a successful drive through dense fog. These gifts of daily life prompt the grace of contemplation, provided that we can see in them the grandeur of God.

Nothing stands outside the transcendent embrace of His love—neither the good times nor the bad, neither the times when we know our direction nor when we feel unsure. All He asks is that we do our best and go on trusting, however tempted we are to give up. What is unclear now will one day be seen in eternity. Then we "will be able to grasp fully, with all the holy ones, the breadth and length and height and depth of Christ's love." We shall "experience this love which surpasses all knowledge, so that [we] may attain to the fullness of God himself" (Eph 3:18–19).

This glorious quotation from St. Paul's Epistle to the Ephesians was on my lips and in my ears as I rode with the family in my father's funeral procession. Instead of the hearse in which we sat, I pictured him approaching his grave in the old red wagon. He would have preferred riding in it, I'm sure, but protocol would not permit it and, for that matter, I doubt if the Wagon could have stood such a sad parting. Our faith told us that Dad was with God, but our sorrow at this moment could not be diminished.

One of the hardest things I have ever had to do was to deliver his eulogy at Mass that morning. The Lord guided my tongue, and, despite the emotion of the moment, I was able to say, in tribute to this hardworking, faithful father:

> The readings for today's liturgy were especially chosen with Dad in mind. He waited upon the Lord in times of darkness with hope. He accepted God's will during a lifetime of loving service. He heard, as does a child, the final appeal of the Father through Jesus and the Holy Spirit: Come to me.
>
> We feel at such moments a painful mixture of emotions. Some expand our heart, others constrict it. We rejoice that Dad no longer suffers from a combination of heart and breathing problems. Yet we weep because he has passed forever from this earthly life.
>
> We feel relief in expressing our feelings to one another and sensing shared sympathy and compassion. Yet we are numbed by the unspeakable depth of this loss, by the pain of words that must go unspoken because he died so suddenly.
>
> We accept the reality of his death with faith and courage. Yet we wonder what this mystery of life and final parting really means.
>
> Dad accepted his death with peace and surrender. Toward the end, before he drew his last few breaths, he raised his arm briefly, as if to acknowledge our presence and our expressions of love. He then lowered it slowly in a gesture of consummation, as if to say, It is over now, I can rest at last, "I have fought the good fight, I have finished the race, I have kept the faith" (2 Tm 4:7).
>
> The meaning of Dad's death—the meaning of any good man's passing—has to be found in the network of relationships that formed his life.
>
> Dad was the son of immigrant parents. He came to this

country when he was six years old. What counted in the
beginning was sheer survival through hard work and sparse
living.

Because of circumstances, Dad never obtained more than a
sixth-grade education, but this did not deter him from working diligently to develop his own home-remodeling business.
He was a self-educated man who obtained his degree, as he
often told me, from the college of hard knocks.

Dad was a friend and a spouse simultaneously. When people called to console mother, I heard her say again and again,
"I've lost my best friend." This is a beautiful sentiment, and I
know it is true. Mother knew Dad as a friend for many years
prior to their marriage. He was a handsome, fun-loving person, with a range of moods from sadness to elation. She loved
them all and knew how to channel them for the good. They
enjoyed forty-one years of married life, giving us a fine home
and a solid Christian upbringing.

My father was a giver of life in many senses. He gave me
and my brothers our physical life, of course. More than this,
he gave us a chance to develop our own diverse personalities,
talents, and professions. I think he was and is proud of his
children, and we know how much we owe to our parents for
their love and support.

Dad was famous for his mixture of gruffness and tenderness, but behind that stubborn exterior beat a heart of gold
that would do anything for his family and his customers. The
laughs we shared far outweighed the bursts of temper.

If I were to choose one main way of remembering Dad, it
would be as a working man, an honest laborer. He had a
wonderful personality for the business world. He made more
friends and acquaintances on his rounds than we could
count. He did lots of favors for his customers and always
preached that they were right, no matter what. He built up
his home-remodeling business, spent hours on the road, and,
during the hard, early years of his marriage, worked around

the clock to provide for our family. His customers still comment today on his gentlemanly presence and on the excellent, enduring quality of his work.

Like many a good layman, he was truly a laborer in the fields. He did not have a big vocabulary, nor did he need it. He knew how to care for people and make them happy. What God hid from the wise and clever, He revealed many times through Dad. He was a great witness, without knowing it, to the beauty of labor lived for the higher purpose of love for God and family.

Toward the end, when he was not able to work, he said that he would rather be dead than to live like this—weak, losing all taste for the enjoyment of food (he who liked to eat with gusto my mother's home cooking), unable to sleep because he could not breathe without wheezing. God in His mercy, knowing this man's limits and strengths, heard his prayer and said, "Come to me, all you who labor and are overburdened, and I will give you rest" (Mt 11:28).

Now the harvesttime has come for Dad. The Lord is spreading the banquet table for this good man, welcoming him as he welcomes all dedicated laborers to the vineyard of glory. Even now, the King is rewarding him for a lifetime of trying to do the best he could for others.

God looks beneath the surface flaws and beholds the inner person: the man who loved and honored my mother in sickness and in health, for richer or poorer; the man who fathered three children and worked hard all his life to provide for us. Now Dad is in heaven to help us get there, too. When life becomes hard and lonely, and the road seems long, I can hear him say, "Keep courage, don't lose heart, fight the good fight until it is finished, never lose your faith in God's good will, live life to the full and live it well." Like Dad, we too shall "wait with silence for the salvation of our God"

(Lam 3:26).

The funeral procession arrived at the burial site. The last ride was over. He came to rest on a low hill between two evergreens. We watched as the soil settled atop the casket, and the workmen closed the grave. We felt an important part of our lives coming to an end. We rode home in silence, because it was too soon to speak of a new beginning. As we drove down the street toward our family home, our eyes focused on the red wagon. We got out and touched her flank, that Old Girl that had carried Dad over so many miles of his journey. It shone in the sun, warm to the touch, as if my father still sat in it. It pleases me to think that when the Wagon went to its own graveyard, Dad came along and retrieved it so that the two of them could ride that fiery red chariot, trailing clouds of glory, straight to heaven.

CLOSING MEDITATION

Life became more precious because our time here on earth is passing. Death awaits us from the moment we are born; then all motion, as we know it, ceases. The turning world stands still. Thoughts, words, images—all fall into impenetrable silence. What lies beyond that final barrier? No one alive knows for sure. We can only rely on the promise of the Lord that our goal is life eternal. In the face of death, especially the death of someone we love, we are led to a meditation on immortality. Anxiety-evoking as it may be, we ought to listen to the counsel of spiritual masters who say, Meditate on your own parting. Let its finality help you to appreciate anew the dear gift of life. Dwell on these last things for a while and listen to what they teach you about the way to live here and now. In the light of these insights, let us pray:

Lord,
Lead me to a meditation
In time on life eternal.
The fulfillment I seek
Can never be found
Amid the fragments
Of earthly existence.
I need meditation
To keep my passing days
In mortal perspective,
To hear in worldly sounds
Your voice most pure.
I feel dispersed
Among dry leaves
Of endless prattle,
Lost in words that touch
Only surface meanings.
Meditation plunges me
Into inner depths
Where night descends,
Handmaiden of your mystery,
Where silence stills
Useless speaking.

Lord,
In quiet meditation
I wait upon your word,
I meet you to whom
In silence I shall one day return.
My true nobility
Is due to your presence in me;
Without you, I accomplish nothing.
Only when your spirit guides me
Can I be your faithful servant,
Called forth to share in your salvation

Until you call me home,
Attentive to you for your sake
And not my own.

Afterword

As we begin to reset the priorities of our life in the direction of the spiritual, we desire increasingly to give God our best moments. We want Him to have nothing less than our most alert presence. Everyone has a different bodily clock. Some are morning people. As soon as they get up, they feel alive, alert, sunny, bubbly. Others feel best in the late afternoon or early evening. The rule is to give priority to the relationship between self and God, for it is only through the power derived from this bond that we can give ourselves to the service of others in the world.

Sadly, we can become so work-oriented—idolizing the "god" of professional competence—that we allow to slip into second place the primary relationship to God. Soon our whole life gets out of kilter. We put participation first, rather than seeing the necessity of establishing a ground of union with the Lord through spiritual practices like reading, meditation, prayer, and contemplation. Out of the ground of being, we flow into doing. We have to reset priorities so that the managing self becomes a servant of the Spirit. Our organizing, functioning capacity will then foster the unfolding of the spiritual life instead of becoming something that is idolized as an end in itself.

Since the renewals associated with Vatican Council II, many external protective structures have been removed, implying that clergy, religious, and laity are being asked to take upon themselves the responsibility for spiritual practices. No one tells us when to do spiritual reading, when to meditate. We have to choose to do these things ourselves. When these external structures are removed in deference to individual responsibility and freedom, the presupposition is that we have to establish internal, freely chosen structures that promote spiritual reading, meditation, and prayer.

If we try to keep up our witness without drinking from the well of Christ's word, we soon dry up. We become mere functionaries. Yet we know that our life is to involve more than mere functioning; it is to radiate Christ to others. How can we radiate what we are not living every day? How can we give what we ourselves do not live? The managing dimension is thus destined to serve our spiritual ideals, helping us to establish internal protective structures that support the primary relationship between us and God.

At the center of this desire to orient our life bodily and functionally to God is the spirit. The spirit self is comparable to the restless heart that finds rest only in God. It keeps reminding us that there is more to life than material gain, more than status, accomplishment, and professional skill. This spirit self is open to the Holy Spirit, who ultimately is the One prompting us to create facilitating conditions for spiritual deepening.

All of these conditions in turn have to be realistically embodied in one's life situation. For instance, a married woman may desire to give herself more personally to God. She realizes that her situation includes spending a great deal of time caring for her husband and children. Perhaps because of financial difficulties, she has to take an extra job. These responsibilities have to be taken into account. Though she may want to set aside half an hour for quiet prayer or formative reading, it may not be possible for her to do so. She has to find other means.

By contrast, a sister living in a contemplative community has more time for such spiritual practices than the average wife or working woman in the world. Her state of life frees her to foster those practices others may not be able to fulfill. These exercises, therefore, have to be taken on in accordance with one's life situation and its consequent commitments.

Many problems affecting the spiritual life today are culturally based. We are products of our culture. In the West, a high premium is placed on the pleasure principle, whether it is manifested in loose sexuality, in drug taking, or in a do-your-own-thing philosophy.

Our culture also puts a high value on the principle of functioning. Retirement crises occur when people find out that they are no longer able to function for health reasons or because of the normal process of aging. Depression sets in. The aged grow isolated and withdrawn; they feel as if they are not worthy anymore, as if they are a burden to their children or to the community. This condition is sad but understandable in a culture that places the highest value on accomplishment and success.

We live in the tension of secularization and spiritualization: secularization with its high esteem of the pleasure principle and its idolatry of doing, and spiritualization with its call to seek union with God, to deepen the life of the spirit, to remember our Maker in the midst of this world, to praise Him, to radiate His truth. These ideals of spiritual deepening are not easy to live by in the kind of world in which we are immersed at the moment.

Spiritual writers and poets have tried to capture in words the tension between secularization and spiritualization. One poet who has done so is T. S. Eliot. In his "Choruses from 'The Rock,'" he writes:

> The endless cycle of idea and action,
> Endless invention, endless experiment,
> Brings knowledge of motion, but not of stillness;
> Knowledge of speech, but not of silence;
> Knowledge of words, and ignorance of the Word.
> All our knowledge brings us nearer to our ignorance,
> All our ignorance brings us nearer to death,
> But nearness to death no nearer to G O D.
> Where is the Life we have lost in living?
> Where is the wisdom we have lost in knowledge?
> Where is the knowledge we have lost in information?
> The cycles of Heaven in twenty centuries
> Bring us farther from G O D and nearer to the Dust.

Eliot describes the secularization of the world basically in terms of forgetfulness. He depicts a world that has forgotten the divine origin of all things, that has made humans and their controlling tendency the measure against which everything else is determined.

In the poet's mind, we live as half persons, hollowed out, unable to hear the Good News. The poet, like the prophets of old, has to raise his voice in the midst of forgetfulness. He has to call us out of loneliness, fragmentation, selfishness, and self-deception. He offers us an opportunity to reassess our values, to look again at the false gods we worship and to see that they cannot fulfill us.

We are children of the light, so why do we live in darkness? If we are children of the light, why are we content with those things that only lead us deeper into darkness? We must awaken from our sleepy deception and turn again toward Him who is the light. We must listen to what He says about relating to His Father, about loving our neighbor, about being faithfully attentive to His word.

In his letter to the Ephesians, St. Paul calls us to wake up from the sleep of our indifference, from our forgetfulness of the sacred, and to remember the divine presence in our midst. His words are these:

> You were darkness once, but now you are light in the Lord; be like children of light, for the effects of the light are seen in complete goodness and right living and truth. Try to discover what the Lord wants of you, having nothing to do with the futile works of darkness but exposing them by contrast. The things which are done in secret are things that people are ashamed even to speak of; but anything exposed by the light will be illuminated and anything illuminated turns into light. That is why it is said:

> > Wake up from your sleep,
> > rise from the dead,
> > and Christ will shine on you. (Eph 5:8–14)

Once we awaken, God opens our eyes to treasures beyond our wildest expectations. Eliot reminds us in this prayer at the end of his poem who we are and who we are called to become:

> In our rhythm of earthly life we tire of light. We are glad when the day ends, when the play ends; and ecstasy is too much pain.
> We are children quickly tired: children who are up in the night and fall asleep as the rocket is fired; and the day is long for work or play.
> We tire of distraction or concentration, we sleep and are glad to sleep,
> Controlled by the rhythm of blood and the day and the night and the seasons.
> And we must extinguish the candle, put out the light and relight it;
> Forever must quench, forever relight the flame.
> Therefore we thank Thee for our little light, that is dappled with shadow.

We thank Thee who hast moved us to building, to finding, to
forming at the ends of our fingers and beams of our eyes.

And when we have built an altar to the Invisible Light, we may
set thereon the little lights for which our bodily vision is
made.

And we thank Thee that darkness reminds us of light.

O Light Invisible, we give Thee thanks for Thy great glory!

It is not easy to be a Christian in today's world. We are
children quickly tired; we are finite, limited, human people.
God understands that we are vulnerable and fragile. He
assures us that we are children. He has implanted in us a
spiritual principle that makes all the difference. Our candle
may be out, but He will forever relight the flame. Such is the
pain and the glory of being human. Therefore, we can thank
Him for our little light that is dappled with shadow. We
thank Him for finding us and forming us in the divine image
and likeness. Most of all, we thank Him that darkness reminds us of light. We give Him thanks for His great glory.

The poet is not telling us that we are angels, nor are we
animals as some would believe. He is not telling us that our
lives will be lived totally in the light, because there is in us
also the darkness of sin. He simply says that the whole point
of the spiritual life is to forever relight the flame. It may go
out because we are human; we may at times be unkind,
complaining, bitter. But, after all, we are light dappled with
shadow. Even that is not the whole story. We are also re-
deemed by Christ from the sleepy complacency of an egocentric existence, and that is what matters most of all.